The Funniest People in Relationships: 250 Anecdotes

David Bruce

Published by David Bruce, 2022.

THE FUNNIEST PEOPLE IN RELATIONSHIPS: 250 ANECDOTES

First edition. October 5, 2022.

ISBN: 979-8215217726

Written by David Bruce.

Table of Contents

Dedication

DEDICATED TO MY SISTER MARTHA

Martha wrote, "When I was working at Longaberger, I worked with a girl who had two children and was in the middle of a divorce. She was so worried about Christmas for her boys. I received a very nice Christmas bonus that year, and I went to my boss and started a donation fund for the girl. My boss told me later that she — my boss —delivered the money to the girl's mother and father and told them not to tell her who brought the money for her. Months later the girl told me that the boys had the best Christmas that year, and she told me someone had brought money to her mom and dad for her, and she went to town and bought the boys Christmas. She never did know who did that for her. She was so thankful. I believe that I was the only one who donated to her, which was just fine."

***

The doing of good deeds is important. As a free person, you can choose to live your life as a good person or as a bad person. To be a good person, do good deeds. To be a bad person, do bad deeds. If you do good deeds, you will become good. If you do bad deeds, you will become bad. To become the person you want to be, act as if you already are that kind of person. Each of us chooses what kind of person we will become. To become a good person, do the things a good person does. To become a bad person, do the things a bad person does. The opportunity to take action to become the kind of person you want to be is yours.

Bai Juyi went to Zen master Daolin of the Tang Dynasty and asked what one must do in order to live in accord with the Tao. Daolin answered, "One must avoid doing evil, and one must do as much good as possible." Bai Juyi was surprised at the simplicity of this answer and said, "Even a child knows that." "True," replied Daolin, "even a child of three knows this but even a man of 80 fails to live up to it."

A seeker after truth once asked a wise person how to seek God. The wise person replied, "The ways to God are as many as there are created beings. But the shortest and easiest is to serve others, not to bother others, and to make others happy."

Cover Photograph for *The Funniest People in Relationships: 250 Anecdotes*

https://pixabay.com/photos/wedding-beach-young-couple-couple-1745240/

All anecdotes have been retold in my own words to avoid plagiarism.

Anecdotes are usually short humorous stories. Sometimes they are thought-provoking or informative, not amusing.

Note: The relationships in this book are of several kinds, not just of Significant Others.

Educate Yourself

Read Like A Wolf Eats

Feel Free to Give This Book to Anyone Free of Charge

Be Excellent to Each Other

Books Then, Books Now, Books Forever

Chapter 1: From Activism to Children

Activism

• Anna Rosenberg, who gave President Franklin Delano Roosevelt the idea for the G.I. Bill of Rights, learned the importance of activism early in life. When she was 14, she was a student at Wadleigh High School in New York City, and she and other students were annoyed because they had to attend school in shifts and share desks because of a lack of desks and other proper facilities. Therefore, she and the other students paid a visit to the city aldermen (politicians), who ignored them because they were a bunch of students. The aldermen even started to leave the room the students were in. However, young Anna yelled after the aldermen, "Very well, gentlemen, you may have heard enough, but now you will hear from our parents, who are your constituents." The aldermen paid attention to the students after that, and Anna told them exactly what the school needed. The next year, each of the students at the school had a desk and attending school in shifts was no longer necessary.[1]

• When African-American poet Nikki Giovanni was a teenager in Knoxville, Tennessee, people gathered together to protest a hate crime. Nikki's grandmother explained that she and Nikki's grandfather were too old to march in the protest — so to take their place in the march they had volunteered Nikki.[2]

Animals

• One of the many dogs in author Gary Paulsen's life was Cookie, the lead dog on his sledding team both in Minnesota and during the 1,049-mile Iditarod Sled Dog Race in Alaska. Cookie arrived in Mr. Paulsen's life lean and hungry, and during his first two days with Mr. Paulsen, Cookie ate a 75-pound beaver carcass. It's a good thing Cookie came into Mr. Paulsen's life. She saved his life at least three times, including once when the ice broke under him and he plunged into an icy lake — Cookie roused the other dogs and they pulled Mr. Paulsen from the water. After Mr. Paulsen decided to give up running sled dogs, he invited Cookie into his house. One of the first things Cookie did was to eat Mr. Paulsen's wife's pet cat. After Cookie died in 1989, Mr. Paulsen dedicated his book *Woodsong* to her.[3]

• Children's book author Betsy Byars has always been very interested in animals, including snakes and bugs. When she was a young girl, she waded in a creek. When she came out, she was very interested to find that brown things had attached themselves to her legs and didn't want to come off, so she went home to show everyone. The brown things were leeches, and her mother was not happy. But despite being forbidden to get leeches on her legs again, Betsy waded in the creek whenever she wanted to collect leeches for a free-admission "zoo" in the backyard.[4]

• In London immediately following World War II, food was scarce. However, one day, Lord Snowy, the pet cat of children's book illustrator Tony Ross's Uncle Barry, came to the rescue. Lord Snowy played on the balcony for a while one day, then dragged a steak into the apartment. Uncle Barry took the steak from Lord Snowy, washed it, and in an exhaustive taste test discovered that it was delicious. Where did the steak come from? No idea. Unfortunately, although Uncle Barry continued to let Lord Snowy play on the balcony, the cat brought no more steaks home.[5]

• Lee Brewster owned and managed Lee's Mardi Gras, a store for cross-dressers (mainly men who dress like women) in New York. He had a beloved house cat named Kitty Cat, and when he had to take his beloved cat to a pet hospital for emergency treatment, he was outraged because the staff placed money before comfort. After Kitty Cat had been treated, the staff would not allow Mr. Brewster to see his beloved cat until he had paid the bill. Mr. Brewster threw his platinum American Express card down and shouted, "Kitty Cat is no pauper!"[6]

• When Paula Klein-Bruno was a kid, she knew that she wanted to be a jockey. She even bought a jockey cap and wore it all the time

— the only way that her mother could get it away from her long enough to clean it was to take it to a one-hour dry cleaner. In 1995, Ms. Klein-Bruno achieved her dream, riding as a jockey in the New York racing circuit. (As a toddler, whenever she saw horse vans on the roads, she would yell, "Horses! Horses!" And as a kid, she often prayed, "God, please don't let me grow too tall." He didn't — she is 4'11".)[7]

• Music director Theodore Stier was with dancer Anna Pavlova as she walked her dog, whose name was Teddy, in Montgomery, Alabama. A man saw them and was greatly impressed with Teddy and asked Mr. Stier if the woman wanted to sell him; however, Ms. Pavlova didn't want to sell such a beloved pet. Therefore, Mr. Stier, Ms. Pavlova, and Teddy continued their walk, only to have the dog-lover suddenly yell to Mr. Stier, "Tell the girl that if only she'll let me have the dog — I'll marry her!"[8]

• American author Flannery O'Connor loved birds all her life. When she was five years old, New York newsreel company Pathé News filmed one of her chickens because it was able to walk backwards. Later, in a home economics class, Flannery created what she described as "a piqué coat with a lace collar and two buttons in the back" for another of her chickens. As an adult, Ms. O'Connor raised peacocks.[9]

• Sir Arthur Sullivan, a conductor, once heard that the young son of soprano Emma Albani was ill. He visited and had tea with Ms. Albani and her young son, who had nearly recovered from his illness. To amuse the boy, Sir Arthur brought a white rabbit, which hopped around the boy's nursery. Thereafter, Ms. Albani's son referred to Sir Arthur as "the White Rabbit."[10]

• Of course, identical triplets are very similar, but they are not so similar that family pets can't tell them apart. For example, Edgar, the dog owned by the family of a set of identical triplets — who are named Darren, David, and Donny — can tell them apart. Their mother can tell Edgar to fetch David, and Edgar knows immediately whom to fetch.[11]

• While she was in the second grade, children's book illustrator Lane Smith entered her pet, Okie, in a dog show at school. Surprisingly, Okie was given a ribbon, and Lane's mother praised Okie and told Lane that everyone was proud of Okie. Lane then looked at the ribbon — it said, "Participation."[12]

• Children's book author and illustrator Dr. Seuss read one newspaper each day. For a while, he subscribed to two newspapers, but the family Irish setter, Cluny, was used to bringing only one newspaper into the house, so she buried the second newspaper.[13]

• Children's book illustrator Maira Kalman is allergic to dogs, so when her children decided that they wanted a dog as a pet, they had to settle for getting a talking bird and teaching it how to bark.[14]

Art

• When American artist Donald Sultan was 11 years old, his parents took him to see the Ringling Museum in Sarasota, Florida. At the circus museum, he saw a work of art titled "The Giant." His mother told him that she had sat on the giant's knee when she was a little girl and that his ring was so big that a half-dollar could pass through it. Mr. Sultan says, "It was at that moment that the art and the magic merged and I decided to be an artist myself."[15]

• Some artists suffer — as do their families. To become an artist, Paul Gauguin gave up a career as a stockbroker. Due to financial difficulties, his wife moved back to her native Denmark. Only occasionally was Mr. Gauguin able to see his children, and when he did, only his two oldest children were able to speak his language: French.[16]

Babies

• As a man of some experience with children, Texas actor Marco Perella knows how to calm babies. One trick he uses is to put the baby's head against his chest, then to hum "Old Man River" in a deep bass. The vibration mesmerizes the baby, making it quiet. While he was doing a TV movie scene for *Murder in the Heartland* with Renée

Zellweger, the baby she was holding started crying. Marco took the baby, hummed "Old Man River" and quieted it, then gave it back to Renée. The baby started crying again. This happened a couple of times, and the director asked what was going on. Renée replied, "This baby hates me." No problem, the director said, they could use a back-up baby in the scene. Unfortunately, the back-up baby behaved exactly the same way as the first baby. Marco hummed "Old Man River" and quieted the baby, then handed it to Renée, and the baby started crying. Eventually, the scene was filmed with Marco holding the baby, and if you listen carefully during the scene, you can hear the humming of "Old Man River."[17]

• Early in her career, when soprano Rita Hunter had a young child, a situation arose suddenly where she needed to be at an important rehearsal and her husband needed to be in a hospital. Having no babysitter because they were so new to the neighborhood, but needing one desperately, she gathered her baby's things, knocked on the door of a neighbor, explained the situation hurriedly, shoved the baby into the neighbor's arms, and ran off. Luck was with her. She hadn't left her daughter in the hands of a dangerous person, but in the hands of a most excellent babysitter, whom she thanked by name — Auntie Symes — in her autobiography, *Wait Till the Sun Shines, Nellie*.[18]

• When Lois Lowry, author of the children's book *Anastasia Krupnik*, was seven years old, she wanted a puppy, so her family arranged to have a puppy delivered as a surprise for her when young Lois was alone at their house. When her family returned home, they discovered Lois sitting on a chest of drawers, afraid of the sharp-toothed puppy. Later, Lois grew used to the puppy, but when it bit her baby brother, her parents said that they had to get rid of it. Lois agreed, but she was surprised when her parents got rid of the puppy — she had thought they were going to get rid of her baby brother.[19]

Baseball

• On November 5, 1988, the National Baseball Hall of Fame in Cooperstown, New York, opened its "Women in Baseball" display, much of which is devoted to the 1940s/1950s All-American Girls Professional Baseball League. Among the women players present for the opening was catcher/outfielder Sarah Jane "Salty" Sands, who brought her 88-year-old father. For more than 30 years, he had boasted about his daughter's accomplishments in professional baseball. Another player, outfielder Lois "Tommie" Barker even chartered a Greyhound bus to transport her supporters to the display opening.[20]

• Nat King Cole was a baseball fan, and his son, Kelly, was a little jealous of the attention that Mr. King gave to baseball. After a tour that had kept Mr. King away from his family, he returned home, but left almost immediately with his wife to attend a Los Angeles Dodgers baseball game. In the ninth inning, the game was tied, and LA fans were hoping for a Dodger hit to win the game, but Kelly simply wanted to see his father. Listening to the game on the radio, Kelly said, "Come on, *anybody*, and get a hit so my mommy and daddy can come home."[21]

• In 1944, Carolyn Morris, a pitcher for the Rockford (Illinois) Peaches team of the All-American Girls Professional Baseball League, saw some boys playing baseball in a sandlot. She asked if she could take a turn at batting. The boys were agreeable, and Ms. Morris promptly hit a home run. Properly impressed, the boys asked her, "Say, lady, have you got a brother who'd like to play ball with us?"[22]

• Baseball manager Joe McCarthy came home discouraged after his Chicago Cubs were defeated. His wife saw his discouragement and said, "You still have me, Joe." Mr. McCarthy smiled, then joked, "Yes, but in the ninth inning today I would have traded you for a sacrifice fly."[23]

• Olympic gold medalist Dot Richardson, a softball shortstop, was discovered when she was a 10-year-old. While she was playing catch with her brother, a man asked her if she wanted to play on his Little

League team, telling her, "We'll cut your hair short and call you Bob."[24]

Birth

• Dr. Rosalyn S. Yalow, a Noble Prize winner, worked at a Veterans Administration hospital which required pregnant women to stop working during the fifth month of pregnancy; however, Dr. Yalow was so valuable to the hospital that the administrators did not want her to stop working. What to do? Answer: Fudge a few documents. According to the official records of the hospital, Dr. Yalow gave birth during the fifth month of two pregnancies — each "five-months-in-the-womb" baby weighed a remarkable 8 pounds, 2 ounces.[25]

• James McNeill Whistler was born in Lowell, Massachusetts, on July 11, 1834. Lowell was then a new town that was devoted to the manufacture of cloth — it was not a classy town. However, Mr. Whistler had the perfect reply when a society lady asked, "Whatever possessed you to be born in a place like that?" He answered, "The explanation is quite simple — I wished to be near my mother."[26]

• Jerry Clower knows that his wife, Homerline, loves him. She had just given birth to a girl, and Mr. Clower, a sports fan, told her, "Honey, we got us a little cheerleader." Homerline, who of course was very tired, looked at him and asked, "Honey, have you had any supper?"[27]

Children

• While growing up in the 1930s, children's book author Tomie dePaola had two grandmothers and one great-grandmother, all of whom were called Nana. To keep them straight, he referred to Nana Upstairs, because his great-grandmother spent all her time upstairs, and Nana Downstairs, because unless this grandmother was helping Nana Upstairs, she could be found downstairs. There was also Nana Fall River, who lived in Fall River, Massachusetts. Nana Upstairs was 94 years old, and she had to be tied to her chair so that she wouldn't fall off the chair. Young Tomie wanted to be like Nana Upstairs, so when he visited her, he requested that he be tied to his chair, too. Nana Downstairs honored the request, but she always tied the knot in front so that he could untie himself when he wanted to wander around. While wandering around, Tomie looked for and often found candy in a sewing box. One day, no candy could be found, so he looked in the medicine cabinet, where he found what he thought was chocolate, which he and Nana Upstairs ate. Unfortunately, the "chocolate" was actually a laxative, and he and Nana Upstairs made messes. After that incident, Nana Downstairs always made sure that there was candy in the sewing box.[28]

• Christina Aguilera became famous at a very young age after coming in second on a nationally televised episode of *Star Search*, being a member of the Disney TV series *Mickey Mouse Club*, and singing the song "Reflection" in the Disney animated movie *Mulan*. Unfortunately, her schoolmates were jealous of her success. After her second-place finish on *Star Search*, someone slashed the tires on her mother's car. Immediately, young Christina transferred to another school. In addition, after newspapers began to print articles about her after she joined the *Mickey Mouse Club*, her new schoolmates resented her success. Fortunately, the resentment of schoolmates was countered by the love of her fans, who started writing her letters, all of which she attempted to answer. After her debut album, *Christina Aguilera*, became a huge success, some young fans who had just bought her record recognized her and bought a disposable camera so they could take her photograph. This kind of attention didn't bother Christina. She said, "I know some people hate that, but not me. I've been waiting for this moment for my entire life."[29]

• Matthew Dunn is the son of David Dunn, who is English, Scottish, and Irish Canadian, and of Morningstar Mercredi, who is Métis (a mixture of French and Native American), Denedeh (a Native American tribe also known as Chipewyan), and Cree (another Native American tribe). When Matthew was three years old, his parents divorced, but they found a unique way for both of them to keep Matthew in their lives. He spends one year with his father in Watrous, Saskatchewan, Canada, then he spends the following year with his mother in Edmonton, Alberta, Canada. By spending alternate years with each parent, Matthew can remain close to each of them. A disadvantage of the arrangement is that Matthew changes schools each year, but an advantage is that he can travel and learn about the cultures of which he is a part. By the way, Matthew has an additional name, courtesy of his Native American heritage. When he was 10 years old, he received the name *Sus Nakáhdul* in a naming ceremony. His Native American name means "Bear Walker."[30]

• Nancy and Rip Talavera used to receive telephone calls each night from the woman who lived in the apartment underneath theirs; she wanted them to tell their daughter to stop jumping in bed so loudly. Nancy and Rip would then check on their daughters. Four-year-old Coral would be sound asleep in her bed, but one-and-a-half-year-old Tracee was jumping in her crib. As you would expect, Tracee grew up to be a gymnast. When she was still very young, she took an acrobatics class and performed in a show while wearing a Mickey Mouse mask. Unfortunately, the mask moved, and she was unable to see out of the eyeholes. She still did the tricks, but she smashed into the back wall, bending one mouse ear. In 1984, Tracee won a silver team medal at the Olympic Games.[31]

• Ezra Jack Keats, author/illustrator of such children's books as *The Snowy Day* and *The Little Drummer Boy*, drew everything he came across when he was a child. One day, he decorated his family's kitchen table with drawings of houses and people. His mother walked into the kitchen, and although he expected to be bawled out for his artwork, she told him, "Did you do that? Isn't it wonderful!" His father, however, worried that being an artist would be a difficult way to make a living, so he wanted his son to do other things, such as play ball. However, when his father realized that Ezra Jack had real talent, he took him on an outing to the Metropolitan Museum in New York City, thus showing that he was proud of his son and his son's talent for art.[32]

• As a child, Trina Schart Hyman, an illustrator of children's books, played at being Little Red Riding Hood. Her mother made her a red satin cape with a hood, and whenever little Trina wore the cape and hood, which was almost every day, her mother also made her a basket of goodies. The path to Grandma's house was in the backyard, her dog was the wolf, and her father was the woodsman who saved Little Red Riding Hood. In her autobiography, *Self-Portrait: Trina Schart Hyman*, Ms. Hyman wrote, "I was Red Riding Hood for a year or more. I think it's a great tribute to my mother that she never gave up and took me to a psychiatrist, and if she ever worried, she never let me know."[33]

• When her children were old enough to go to school, Eve Bunting started to write books in a room in the attic. When she wanted to write, she warned her children not to interrupt her unless it was an emergency. Despite the warning, she was frequently interrupted. A child would appear at the bottom of the stairs and yell up at her, "It's an emergency! I can't find my shoes!" One day, one of her children yelled, "It's a true emergency! Come see the drawing I did! It's really good!" Despite the interruptions, Ms. Bunting managed to write and have published *The Two Giants* — and 100 other books for children.[34]

• When children's book author Tomie dePaola was growing up, his mother brushed her hair and put on her makeup while sitting in front of a vanity, which made her feel a little silly because, as she pointed out, she was not a movie star. However, her little boy, Tomie, did want to look like a movie star, so one day he sat in front of the vanity and put on his mother's lipstick, trying to look like his favorite movie star: Mae West. When he tried to remove the lipstick, he couldn't, so his family found out what he had done. For a few days, little Tomie ran around the neighborhood with brightly colored lips.[35]

• Opera singer Leo Slezak used to take his children to an amusement park where they would hit Punchy Monkey — a large robot with a well-padded face — on the jaw. Punchy Monkey would growl when you hit him, the volume of the growl depending on the intensity with which you hit him. Often, Mr. Slezak played Punchy Monkey with his children at home, letting them hit him gently, then growling. One morning, Mr. Slezak was still asleep when his very young daughter walked into his bedroom and hit him in the face. When he woke up angry, she explained, "I thought you were playing Punchy Monkey."[36]

• As a child, Benjamin West made his own paint brushes, using hairs from the tail of the family cat. Unfortunately, Benjamin liked to paint, and soon the cat's tail had bald places. A visitor from Philadelphia saw Benjamin's works of art and was so impressed that he gave him some paints and brushes. Because Benjamin enjoyed painting so much, he played hooky from school and instead went into the attic to paint. His parents had no idea he was playing hooky until his teacher paid a visit to find out where Benjamin had been for the last several school days.[37]

• Bonnie Blair's family were speed skaters. In fact, when Bonnie was born, her father and siblings were at the ice rink doing exactly that. Bonnie's birth was even announced over the ice rink loudspeaker in this way: "Another speed skater has been born to the Blair family." The announcement was true. When Bonnie was two years old, she started skating — her siblings acquired the smallest pair of skates they could find and slipped them over Bonnie's regular shoes. As an Olympic speed skater, Bonnie won five gold medals.[38]

• R.L. Stine, author of the *Fear Street* and *Goosebumps* series, used to listen to the beginning of the *Suspense* radio show when he was a child. The show opened with a gong being struck, then a scary voice said, with appropriate pauses, "And now ... tales ... calculated ... to keep you ... in *suspense*." The opening of the show was so scary that young

Bob used to turn off the radio and not listen to the rest of the show. As an adult, Mr. Stine says, "Today, I try to make my books as scary as that announcer's voice."[39]

• In kindergarten, future author Frank DeCaro met a little girl named Heidi who loved to play a joke on her friends. She would say, "Let's see who can hit the lightest." After her friend had lightly tapped her arm, she would hit him as hard as she could, then laugh and say, "I lose." In the first grade, Frank went to the hospital to have his tonsils removed, so Heidi wrote him this note: "I like you and you like me. I will buy you a toy." According to Mr. DeCaro, "At six, that was my idea of love."[40]

• Impressionist painter Edgar Degas loved children. A mother once criticized her daughter for making spelling mistakes, then she asked Mr. Degas, "It's very bad to misspell, is it not, Monsieur Degas?" He agreed, but when the mother's back was turned, he asked the child, "Which would you prefer — to spell correctly and not have ice cream or to make mistakes and have ice cream?" The child replied, "To make mistakes and have ice cream." Mr. Degas agreed, "So would I."[41]

• When Julie Krone was two years old, a woman came to her family's farm to look at a horse she was thinking about buying. To show that the horse was gentle, her mother lifted young Julie up and put her on the back of the horse, then she started talking to the woman. As she was talking, the horse trotted off. Her mother was understandably worried, but young Julie grabbed the reins and turned the horse around. As an adult, Ms. Krone became a famous jockey.[42]

• When Jamie Tevis, wife of Walter Tevis (author of the novels *The Hustler*, *The Color of Money*, and *The Man Who Fell to Earth*) was about to give birth to their first child, Will, the pain of the contractions made her say, "I can't go through with this." Her husband replied, "It's too late to think about that now." When Will became a toddler, a favorite activity was hearing his mother sneeze. This made him laugh so hard that he would fall down.[43]

• As a kid growing up in the 1950s, Newbery Award-winning author Jerry Spinelli sometimes attended movies in the park. According to tradition, teenagers sat on the benches while young kids such as Jerry sat on the ground. One evening, Jerry decided to sit on a bench. This went well until some teenagers decided that they wanted to sit on the bench. They lifted one end of the bench into the air — and Jerry slid off the other end.[44]

• Children's book author Joanna Cole uses in her books things that have happened in her family. For example, in one book, a child finds a "rock" that is actually a piece of Styrofoam covered with dirt. In real life, Joanna's daughter, Rachel, was so excited to discover such a "rock" at the park that she had told Joanna, "Mommy, Mommy, look at this *terrific* rock." Joanna couldn't bring herself to tell Rachel that it wasn't a rock.[45]

• Susan Butcher grew up in Cambridge, Massachusetts, but she disliked the noise, confusion, and lack of open space. When she was in the first grade, she even wrote a paper with the title "I Hate Cities." (The title was also the entire paper.) She also asked her parents to allow her to live in a tent in their yard. As an adult, she moved to Alaska, where she won the 1,049-mile Iditarod dog sled race multiple times.[46]

• During Canadian winters, Canadian schoolchildren wear snowsuits. A kindergarten teacher once dressed one of her students in a snowsuit that was loaded with buttons and zippers, so he could go outside for recess. After she dressed him, he told her, "This isn't my snowsuit," so she undressed him again. After she had undressed the boy, he told her, "This snowsuit's my sister's, but my mom said I could wear it today."[47]

• Even in her youth, opera singer Geraldine Farrar exhibited assertiveness. Clarence, a 12- or 13-year-old boy who was older than she, tripped her with his hockey stick. Although she told him to stop, he continued. After he had tripped her three times, she removed three metal ribs from her umbrella, then taught him a lesson that resulted in his being unable to sit down without pain for a few days.[48]

• Children's author Eve Bunting was born in an old Irish house that her father and grandfather had also been born in. Before it was a house, it had been a granary, and because the house was so old, it sometimes settled, sending a shower of seeds down from the ceiling onto the residents. Young Eve thought that ghosts were playing tricks on her family, so she would look upward and yell, "You up there! Stop that!"[49]

• As a child, E.L. Konigsburg, author of *From the Mixed-Up Files of Mrs. Basil E. Frankweiler*, suffered from a case of what her family referred to as "dishes diarrhea." When it was time to do the dishes, she disappeared into the bathroom with some reading material. When she read the end of *Gone with the Wind*, she cried. Because she didn't want anyone to hear her crying, she flushed the toilet again and again.[50]

• Children's book author Sid Fleischman lived much of his youth in San Diego, California, where snow was a rarity, if not an impossibility. When he was very young, his father drove him and his three-year-old sister, Honey, to the mountains so they could see snow and play in it. Unfortunately, Honey was so scared of the snow that she started crying and refused to get out of the car and play in the snow.[51]

• Popular children's author Gary Paulsen once spoke on a panel at a Minnesota college where everyone was very polite. Suddenly, a group of middle-school students — all of them fans of Mr. Paulsen's books — rushed in and started peppering him with questions about his books and characters. Pleased, Mr. Paulsen says, "Everyone had been so proper before, and the kids just blew it wide open!"[52]

• Children's book illustrator Pat Cummings started drawing with crayons when she was very young. Often, she would take a drawing to her mother, who would say something like, "What a nice duck." Young Pat would say that it wasn't a duck, and her mother would look at the drawing more closely and say, "Oh, I see. It's a dinosaur." Pat would then reveal, "It's a picture of Daddy."[53]

• Benjamin West, the son of a Quaker family, demonstrated exceptional artistic ability as a child. This worried the Quakers, who chose to live simply; in fact, many Quakers did not have any pictures in their houses. Therefore, his parents discussed young Benjamin's talent with the church elders, who decided that God gave his talent to him and so he ought to develop it.[54]

• Comedian Flip Wilson started acting at age nine in a school play about Clara Barton. The girl who was supposed to play Clara Barton got sick, and since Flip was the only child who knew Clara Barton's lines, he played her. He said that it was a thrill to have that many lines because originally he was going to play a wounded soldier who did nothing but groan.[55]

• Even as a child, Hugh Troy enjoyed playing practical jokes. His next-door neighbor owned a cherry tree that he was very proud of. When the neighbor went on vacation, Hugh Troy bought a few bushels of apples and tied the apples to the cherry tree branches. The neighbor called in several people to see the "miracle" before discovering the practical joke.[56]

• Brinton Turkle dedicated his first book, *Obadiah the Bold*, to his youngest son, Jonathan. Mr. Turkle pointed out that the book would be read in libraries all across the United States and Jonathan's name would appear in the front of the book. Jonathan was nonchalant about the honor, merely saying, "OK, Daddy. I don't mind."[57]

• Mr. and Mrs. Perry Schwartz adopted two children — a boy and a girl, who were not related by birth — from Honduras. They brought the girl home on March 25, and a couple of years later they brought the boy home on March 23. Each year, the Schwartz family celebrates "Gotcha Day" — March 24 — by doing something special.[58]

• Children's book author/illustrator David McPhail enjoyed creating art even when he was very young. One day, he loaded up his little red wagon with lots of drawings he had created and dragged them off to show his little girlfriend. What happened to the drawings? Mr. McPhail thinks that his girlfriend's mother burned them.[59]

• When she was a child, children's book illustrator Amy Schwartz borrowed and read many library books. At one point, she borrowed and read books by authors whose names began with W, Y, and Z because she thought that books from that section of the children's library were more advanced than the other books.[60]

• James M. Barrie, author of *Peter Pan*, loved children. He sometimes used to go on walks with young children and find a peapod in a hollow tree. He would tell the children that the peapod contained a letter written by a fairy and when he opened the peapod, sure enough, he found a tiny letter that he read to the children.[61]

• Mary Cassatt loved to paint children, but sometimes they did not want to be her models. One of her nephews, Gardner, Jr., appeared in her painting, *Boy in a Sailor Suit*, but at one point he grew tired of posing and spat in her face. The boy's mother locked him in a closet as punishment, but Mary bought him a box of chocolates.[62]

• One Sunday, Virginia K. Barnes sat behind the pastor's wife and son. Before the sermon, the son asked his mother if he could be excused to go to the nursery, but his mother said that he was six years old and too old to go to the nursery. The son protested, "But, Mom, I heard it [the sermon] last night and it's a long one."[63]

• As a youngster, Buster Keaton was thrown about on stage by his vaudevillian parents. In real life, he was also thrown about. When he was three years old, a cyclone picked him up — sucking him right out of a hotel window — whirled him around for a little while, then deposited him safely on the ground.[64]

• Clifford Goldsmith was the original author of *The Aldrich Family*, a radio program about the troubles of teenager Henry Aldrich. Mr. Goldsmith frequently used the antics of his own children in his plots for the program, and he claimed to worry that his own children might sue him for plagiarism.[65]

• J.K. Rowling, author of the Harry Potter books, enjoyed the TV cartoon series *Animaniacs*. When her daughter Jessica was small, Ms. Rowling asked her to wake her up when *Animaniacs* came on early Saturday morning. Jessica did so by gleefully jumping up and down on her mother's bed.[66]

• As a child, Amy Tan, author of *The Joy Luck Club*, wanted to fit in with the children in her neighborhood, so for a week she wore a clothespin on her nose as she slept in an attempt to make it look more American and less Chinese. The only thing that happened was that her nose got sore.[67]

• When she was two years old, J.K. Rowling, the author of the Harry Potter books, got a baby sister: Dianne. Her parents gave J.K. some Play-Doh while they took care of Dianne. J.K. did exactly what any typical two-year-old would do when given some Play-Doh — she ate it.[68]

• When Walter and Jamie Tevis moved to New Haven, Connecticut, a four-year-old girl came over to talk to them. Mr. Tevis asked, "Little girl, would your mother want you to be visiting strangers?" The little girl answered, "You're not strangers. I know you now."[69]

• Opera singer Leo Slezak and his wife were very conscientious about the health of their children. Whenever the Slezak family ate in restaurants, the parents ordered boiling hot water and washed all the silverware before allowing their children to eat.[70]

• George Inness, an important American landscape artist, was totally devoted to his work. One day, a visitor asked him how many children he and his wife, Lizzie, had, and Mr. Inness didn't know! He replied, "Lizzie will be here soon. She knows."[71]

• Theodore Roosevelt's daughter, Alice, was a terror. When her father was the President of the United States, little Alice enjoyed telling visitors to the White House that her father beat his children each and every day. (She was lying.)[72]

• Dorothy Hamill's autobiography, *On and Off the Ice*, contains some photographs her parents took of her when she was a baby and when she was a very young girl. The photographs are labeled, "Early publicity shots."[73]

• Children's book illustrator Floyd Cooper has a son named Dwayne. When Dwayne was very small, he was very talented at rolling over, so Mr. Cooper thought, "Great! We don't need a pet!"[74]

• Identical triplets David, Donny, and Darren are very close. When they were babies, they wouldn't fall asleep until they were placed so close together that they were touching.[75]

• When Lisa, actor Jack Gilford's daughter, was a little girl, she signed a statement that said, "I am having a happy childhood."[76]

Chapter 2: From Christmas to Easter

Christmas

• As a child, Trina Schart Hyman, an illustrator of children's books, believed in fairies. So did her kid sister, Karleen. When Karleen started asking for a real fairy, Trina decided to give her one. She bought a celluloid doll, glued some of her mother's long red-gold hair to it, and painted big, blue eyes on it. She also glued the wings of a Monarch butterfly to the doll's shoulders. In addition, she started writing letters from the fairy and left them on Karleen's pillow. The first letter said, "My name is Kloraine, and I am a lost fairy. I am trying to find my way to your house." Karleen believed the letter and spoke in whispers the day she received it. She was also very happy to wake up one day and find Kloraine on her night table. Later, another lost fairy named Lacey joined the family, and the two girls and the two fairies had many wonderful adventures together. Long after Trina and Karleen stopped believing in fairies, Kloraine and Lacey stayed in the family. Each December, they appeared as ornaments on the family Christmas tree.[77]

• Ben, a young nephew of lesbian humorist Ellen Orleans, wanted a Barbie for Christmas, but not for his birthday, because he didn't want the other kids to see what he was getting. Ms. Orleans was a little surprised by the request, and she asked her sister-in-law about it. As it happened, the sister-in-law didn't particularly like her son's desire in toys, but only because she regards Barbie as a sexist toy. Ms. Orleans ended up buying her nephew a Barbie with two outfits: a white satin dress and a cowboy outfit — the cowboy outfit had actually been created for Barbie's boyfriend, Ken. She sent it to her nephew in a box marked "Private! For Ben Only!" She also enclosed this note: "Remember, Ben, in real life women do not have permanently arched feet." Later, she received a note from her sister-in-law about the gift:

"Great minds think alike. I bought Ben a Dancin' Barbie. He's in heaven."[78]

• When Alyene Porter was a little girl growing up early in the 20th century, a man named Brother Mahoney in her church had a distinctive and chronic case of the sniffles: He would make one big sniffle, pause, then make three small sniffles in a row. There was never any variation in his sniffling. On Christmas Eve, little Alyene was getting ready to talk to Santa Claus at the church when she heard Santa give a sniffle that sounded just like the sniffle of Brother Mahoney. To make sure, she listened closely: one big sniffle, pause, then three small sniffles in a row. Shocked and disappointed, she ran crying to her mother, who explained that anyone can be Santa Claus as long as they like children and spread joy at Christmas. That night, Alyene's parents woke her so she could be Santa and help fill the Christmas stockings while her siblings slept.[79]

• On the live TV program *The Garry Moore Show*, Mr. Moore decided to see what kind of Christmas gifts young children really prefer. Therefore, he filled the stage with gifts ranging from very expensive to very inexpensive, then he brought two eight-year-olds — a boy and a girl — out on stage and invited them to choose one gift for their very own. The boy chose a sled, even though he lived in Florida. When Mr. Moore asked the boy if he had ever seen it snowing in Florida, he replied, "No, but this year I'm hoping it will." The little girl walked past a very expensive dollhouse with working lights and instead chose an inexpensive stuffed doll. Later, she explained, "I picked my doll because she looked so lonely."[80]

• When she was a child, E.L. Konigsburg, author of *From the Mixed-Up Files of Mrs. Basil E. Frankweiler*, could not sing well. Her elementary school class was divided into bluebirds and redbirds. The bluebirds sang, and the redbirds listened. Young Elaine was a redbird. However, at Christmas, the redbirds were allowed to sing carols. Young

Elaine wanted to sing, so she did, but because she was Jewish, whenever a carol referred to "Jesus" or "Christ," she hummed.[81]

• When Ivan Jadan, the premier lyric tenor of the Bolshoi Opera from 1928-1941, was three years old, he received a beautiful toy horse on wheels for a Christmas present. He had been taught to keep himself and his possessions clean, so one day soon after Christmas, he grabbed a brush and wheeled his horse to the river to wash it. Unfortunately, his horse was made of papier-mâché, and after he had washed it, nothing was left but the wheels.[82]

• On Christmas day, 1911, artist Louise Bourgeois was born in Paris. Of course, everyone was celebrating Christmas, and the doctor who delivered Louise told her very apologetic mother, "Madame Bourgeois, really, you are ruining my festivity."[83]

• When Isaac Newton was born on Christmas Day, 1642, the two women helping his mother thought he would die quickly, so when they went out to get him medicine, they didn't hurry back. Instead, they sat on a wall and rested.[84]

Couples

• Stand-up comedian Fran Capo made her fiancée learn what it was like to be a stand-up comedian before they were married. He killed the first time he did his act, so she made him do it again. This time, he bombed. Figuring that he knew what the extremes of a stand-up's life were like, she said, "OK, now you can stop." She also made him appear in a movie with her — they both were extras, and he was made up as a punk carrying a doll penetrated by a knife. They took a photograph together, which he sent to his mother with the note, "This is the girl I am going to marry." Ms. Capo says, "She was thrilled."[85]

• Norman Lear, who revolutionized television sitcoms in the 1970s, wanted to propose to his then-girlfriend, Lyn, as they were vacationing in Kauai. She was very relaxed, lying in a hammock, and Mr. Lear knew he shouldn't disturb her, but he was so nervous he decided to propose right then. Unfortunately, although he is a writer, the right words would not come to him. He said, with increasing desperation, "How can I show you? How can I tell you? WHAT CAN I DO?" Lyn, who was busy relaxing, replied, "You can leave me the f —k alone."[86]

• Hispanic movie actor Antonio Banderas has been successful at avoiding the stereotype of the Latin lover in Hollywood, although he is handsome, successful, and sexy. In real life, he has sometimes been unsuccessful in his pursuit of females. Once, he got down on one knee and declared his love for a girl, and she ignored him. (Of course, he was only five years old then.)[87]

• One of ballerina Darci Kistler's best roles has been that of Princess Aurora in Tchaikovsky's *Sleeping Beauty*. When she first learned that she had gotten the role, her mother told her, "Now your prince will come." A few months afterward, Ms. Kistler married dancer Peter Martins.[88]

• Lesbian comedian Suzy Berger tells audiences that on her answering machine is this message: "You're reached the home of Suzy Berger and Jodie Foster." When the audience members laugh, she stares at them and says, "It could happen."[89]

Daughters

• As the author of the Harry Potter books, J.K. Rowling frequently travels from book signing to book signing. However, often she is too busy signing her autograph and meeting with her fans to see the sights in some of the places she visits. During a trip to Seattle, Jessica, her six-year-old daughter, was gleeful because she was able to go up in the Space Needle and her mother couldn't because she was too busy.[90]

• When Paul Krassner's 16-year-old daughter lost her virginity, she let him know by calling him on the telephone and playing Carly Simon's "Daddy, I'm Not a Virgin Anymore." His emotions were conflicting. On the one hand, he was proud that she had found an original way of letting him know that she was entering into a new phase of her life. On the other hand, he was jealous because he was still a virgin at her age.[91]

• Sometimes, opera singers carry on snatches of conversation during live performances. While they were performing in *Aida*, Zinka Milanov whispered to George London, "George, how's the new baby? I understand she's a darling."[92]

Death

• While attending school at Exeter, Robert Benchley was required to write a paper on a practical subject—he choose to write on the topic of embalming and even did research, interviewing a local undertaker. Later, when humorist George Ade died, the adult Benchley got out of bed and went out and had a good time, telling stories about Mr. Ade and drinking. According to Mr. Benchley, "When a great humorist dies, everybody should go to a place where there is laughter, and drink to his memory until the lights go out." When Mr. Benchley died, his will, in which he left everything to his wife, was exactly one sentence long: "Confident that she will adequately provide for our two sons, and any child hereafter born to us, I make no provision for them, but give all my property to Gertrude D. Benchley, absolutely, appointing her Executrix without security."[93]

• As English National Opera soprano Leslie Garrett's grandfather lay dying in a hospital, one of his nurses discovered that Ms. Garrett was his granddaughter. The nurse exclaimed, "Gosh, Leslie Garrett's the most famous opera singer in the country." Her grandfather sat up and told the nurse with his last words, "The world, young lady — she's the most famous in the world!"[94]

• A tourist approached the driver of a horse-drawn carriage in Central Park and asked, "How many people can you take?" The driver answered, Five." The tourist said, "But I have a family of six." The driver replied, "What do you want me to do about it? Shoot one of them?"[95]

• At the Russian funeral of her husband, Sergei Grinkov, Ekaterina Gordeeva carried a bouquet of wilted red and yellow flowers. They were the last thing he had given to her before dying unexpectedly of a heart attack on November 20, 1995, in Lake Placid, New York.[96]

• For a while, Wilson Mizner worked in Hollywood, adding gags to comedy scripts. While working on the screenplay of *The Merry Wives of Reno*, Mr. Mizner learned that his brother Addison was dying, so he telegraphed him, "Stop dying. Am trying to write a comedy."[97]

Easter

• When children's book illustrator Lisa Campbell Ernst was young, her family had a pet dog named Heidi. Heidi had a good appetite, but she often hid part of her food so she could eat it later. Because she was an indoor dog, she hid food in the family's furniture — Lisa's father once found a pancake hidden in his favorite chair. One Easter, Lisa and her siblings received three beautiful Easter baskets filled with candy and eggs. Of course, they left the baskets at home while they attended church, and when they returned, they found that Heidi had gotten into the Easter baskets, eaten a good deal of the edibles, and hidden the rest. The Easter hunt was decidedly non-traditional that year, as the family found candy and eggs hidden all over the house. Even though the children couldn't eat the candy and eggs, they still felt that Heidi had made a wonderful Easter bunny.[98]

Chapter 3: From Education to Friends

Education

• When children's book author Betsy Byars was three years old, she heard a lot about Miss Harriet, the first-grade teacher of her older sister, and she couldn't wait to grow up and be a student in Miss Harriet's class, so that she could paint and be read to from a book titled *The Adventures of Mabel*. Betsy did grow old enough to go to school, and on the first day, she and the other students were assigned to various teachers. Unfortunately, Betsy was not assigned to Miss Harriet. Nevertheless, she knew what she wanted, and she went to Miss Harriet's class anyway. Soon, the principal appeared in the classroom, looking for her, since she had not gone to the right room. Betsy told the principal, "I want to be in Miss Harriet's room." Then she corrected herself and said, "I have to be in Miss Harriet's room." Miss Harriet told the principal, "Let her stay." The principal did, and first grade with Miss Harriet was as wonderful as Betsy had hoped it would be.[99]

• As a teenager, American artist Audrey Flack wanted to be accepted into New York City's High School of Music and Art. She was asked to bring her works of art in a portfolio to the high school and to take an art exam. Since she didn't know what a portfolio was, she went to a dime store. There she discovered an eight-by-ten brown folder marked "PORTFOLIO." She bought it, removed the pieces of stationery from inside it, and put her own drawings inside. When her father drove her to the high school, she saw art students carrying large leather cases and realized that those must be real portfolios. She was so embarrassed that she didn't want to get out of the car. Fortunately, her father pushed her out, she took the exam and passed, and she became first an art student and then a noted artist.[100]

• In November of 1973, Soviet gymnast Olga Korbut competed in the all-around competition at the European Championships. She performed well, but fellow Soviet gymnast Ludmilla Tourischeva performed better, winning gold to Olga's silver. When the medal winners were walking to the awards platform, Olga suddenly turned away, walked to a bench, and sat down. She was so disappointed in coming in second that she wanted to refuse to accept the silver medal. However, a female Soviet coach walked over to Olga, grabbed her shoulders, and marched her back to the line. Olga accepted the silver medal and learned something about showing grace when coming in second.[101]

• When children's book author Tomie dePaola first walked into his kindergarten classroom, he asked the teacher, "When do we learn to read?" She explained that students didn't learn to read in kindergarten, but they would learn to read the following year, in first grade. Tomie replied, "Fine, I'll be back next year." Then he went home. The school called his parents — his father was working and his mother was shopping. His parents found him at home, looking at a book, trying to figure out how to read it. His mother then explained that he needed to pass kindergarten in order to go to the first grade, where he would learn to read, and so Tomie reluctantly attended kindergarten.[102]

• When gymnast Tracee Talavera was a schoolchild, she used to teach acrobatics to the children in the special class — that is, children who were blind or deaf — during recess. She would line the children up and have them do handstands and cartwheels and other forms of tumbling. Since the blind children could hear, she would yell at them and tell them what to do, and she learned a little sign language so she could communicate with the deaf children. She remembers one particular deaf boy who could hold a handstand seemingly forever. She also remembers one particular blind girl who was very smart — "She used to steal my lunch and eat it when I wasn't looking!"[103]

• When soprano Leslie Garrett was very young and had just started to attend grammar school, her pet rabbit died. She was distraught and did not attend school the day she and her family held a funeral for her pet rabbit. The following day, she returned to school, bearing a note from her mother that explained the reason for her absence. Young Leslie worried about what her mother had written, since she realized that school authorities would not regard the death of a rabbit as a suitable reason for not attending school. Fortunately, her mother had simply written, "Family Bereavement."[104]

• Richard A. Watson, a professor of philosophy at Washington University, refuses to have a television set in his home. He relates in his book *Good Teaching* that this used to upset his young daughter, Anna, because when she said she wanted to watch TV, he told her to go to someone else's house. However, when Anna became a college student, she began to think that her father had been right to keep TV out of their home. At her university, she discovered that many students were watching TV four to six hours a day, and she wondered when they found time to study.[105]

• The father of Robert Newton Peck, author of such young people's novels as *A Day No Pigs Would Die*, was a Shaker — a member of a pacifist religious group who practiced simple living. Robert was the only child to go to school, and actually, his parents didn't want him to go to school. His teacher realized this, and when she met Robert's father, she told him, "Thank you for giving me Robert. I shall try to be deserving of your trust." Robert's father replied, "Whatever he breaks, I'll pay for."[106]

• Richard A. Watson, the author of *Good Teaching*, has a sister named Connie, who wanted to go to college. Unfortunately, she never managed to go and so ended up in the type of job a high-school graduate usually ends up in. Whenever a college student in the company she works for moans and groans about bad teaching at the university, she looks the student in the eye and asks, "You want to end up at my age with a job like mine?"[107]

• Phyllis Reynolds Naylor, the author of such children's books as *Shiloh* and *The Agony of Alice*, loved making up stories even when she was in kindergarten. One day, her kindergarten teacher asked each of her students to make up a story, which she would write down. Young Phyllis dictated her story, then stood in line again to dictate a second story, then stood in line again to dictate a third story. Finally, her teacher told her that that was "quite enough turns for one day!"[108]

• When Jason, Candy Chester's son, was three years old, the church they attended began to meet in a local school while waiting to move into a new building. Both the school and the church had folding chairs, so to keep the chairs from being mixed up, church members painted "Jesus" on the church's folding chairs. One day, Jason said that he could spell the word "chair," then he spelled "J-E-S-U-S."[109]

• When he was in the third grade, Newbery Award-winning author Jerry Spinelli wore his cowboy outfit — complete with hat, guns, jodhpurs, and spurs — to school. His teacher took the outfit in stride and asked, "Jerry, would you like to do something for us?" Young Jerry went up in front of the class and sang, "I Got Spurs That Jingle Jangle Jingle." As accompaniment for himself, he shook his spurs.[110]

• Even as a 14-year-old youngster, entertainer Jennifer Lopez took her craft seriously. During a dance class, her teacher saw that she looked upset as she struggled during class. Thinking that she had boyfriend trouble, he asked her what was wrong. She replied, "I just want to be better." Impressed by her seriousness about dance, he replied, "You will."[111]

• When she was a little girl, J.K. Rowling, author of the Harry Potter books, enjoyed her first day of school, but she was surprised that she had to go back to school — she thought that after she had gone one day, she had finished school and she never needed to go back.[112]

• For a while, computer guru Bill Gates went to an all-boys' private school named Lakeside. When the school went co-ed, Mr. Gates programmed the school's computer to give him a schedule that made him the only boy in classes filled with girls.[113]

Fathers

• Edward Jenner wanted to find a vaccine to prevent smallpox. He had learned that people who had contracted cowpox or swinepox were immune to the disease, so he decided to experiment to see if deliberately giving people the mild diseases of cowpox or swinepox would keep them from contracting the deadly disease of smallpox. He would have used himself as a guinea pig, but he had previously recovered from smallpox and so had acquired immunity. Therefore, he gave his own son swinepox, then later injected him with smallpox. The smallpox had no effect on his son. This experiment led to the adoption of vaccines to fight smallpox and saved an enormous number of lives.[114]

• When children's book author Lois Lowry was nine years old, she wanted a man's woolen hunting shirt she frequently looked at in a shop window. Her father noticed that she wanted the shirt, and so he took her into the store to try it on. Of course, even the smallest size was much too large for her, but her father bought it for her anyway. In her autobiography, *Looking Back: A Book of Memories*, Ms. Lowry writes, "I wore it for years. I loved that shirt. I loved my father for buying it for me. I loved the entire world for being the kind of world where such a shirt, and such a father, existed." She also recognizes that buying the shirt was practical — she never outgrew it.[115]

• Emilio Diaz, the father of actress Cameron Diaz, was a true sports nut, and he taught his two daughters, Chimene and Cameron, to love sports, too. When he woke up on Sunday mornings when his daughters were young, even before he raised his head from his pillow, he would shout, "FOOTBAAALLLL." He also teased his two daughters by telling them occasionally to go and play on the freeway. Of course, they understood that he was joking. Cameron and her parents have a good relationship, and she even decided to quit smoking to set a better example after her parents pointed out that they had seen her smoking in seven of her movies.[116]

• Comic singer Anna Russell once did some nude modeling — artistic, not pornographic. (The photographer's wife and female assistant were always present during the photo sessions.) Ms. Russell had a nice figure, although she did not care for her face so much — but then, the photographer did not take photographs of her face. One of the photographs appeared in a London newspaper, where her father saw it, but fortunately he did not recognize her. After looking at the photograph, her father remarked, "It's amazing what people will stoop to for money."[117]

• Comedian Robert Klein's father never ate vegetables because he thought salad was a dish fit only for cows. As a result, his bowel movements were infrequent. Once, when Robert was young, the urge suddenly came on his father, who dashed for the bathroom. Immediately, he yelled for Robert to bring him an umbrella. Robert did as he was told, and when he opened the door to the bathroom, he saw his father sitting on the throne, and above his father, hanging on a clothesline, were his mother's dripping undergarments.[118]

• One way for a man to become a feminist is to have a daughter who is a feminist. In 1854, Elizabeth Cady Stanton spoke to the legislature of New York about women's rights, saying, "We ask no better laws than those you have made for yourselves … simply on the ground that the rights of every human being are the same and identical." Before she gave her speech, she read it to her father, who was a respected jurist. At first, her father threatened to disinherit her, but eventually he helped her with the speech's legal analysis.[119]

• Once, when her father was visiting her, lesbian comedian Kate Clinton invited some of her friends over for dinner. She did establish one conversational rule ahead of time (for her own comfort) — no talk about gay sex. As the dinner progressed, she and her friends discussed such topics as gay politics and gay theory, and at the end of the dinner, she turned toward her father and asked, "What do you think we as gay people can do to make more bridges to straight people?" Her father paused, then answered, "Keep talking."[120]

• H. Allen Smith's father had many, many children. Whenever he wanted to read his newspaper, his numerous small children tearing around the house bothered him. Therefore, he invented a game to keep them quiet. One day he pulled a penny from his pocket, told his children to watch him, then he rubbed the coin on a rug until it shone like new. After that, whenever he wanted some peace and quiet, he would give each of his children a penny and tell them, "Go shine."[121]

• Aretha Franklin remained unspoiled despite becoming a rhythm and blues superstar with numerous Grammy Awards. She credits her father with ensuring that she did not become spoiled. At home, everyone in her family would be working — vacuuming, washing dishes, etc. — but young Aretha would sometimes stand around, doing nothing. Whenever this happened, her father would tell her, "See if you can find yourself around in that kitchen and introduce yourself to the trash."[122]

• When Shaquille O'Neal was 13 years old, he stood 6 feet, 6 inches tall and was growing so fast that new clothes became too small for him after only a few weeks. However, his size by itself did not make him a good basketball player. When Shaq was a high-school senior, his father criticized him, saying that he wasn't playing hard enough. This criticism so motivated Shaq that in the very next game he scored 52 points.[123]

• When Casey Stengel was a young man, he smashed an inside-the-park home run, but his shoelace came untied as he ran around the bases. The loose shoe made him run awkwardly, and he ended up staggering across home base. In the stands sat his fiancée, Edna Lawson, and her father. Proud of the home run, Ms. Lawson asked her father, "What do you think of my hero now, Pa?" Unimpressed with Casey's base running, her father replied, "I just hope he lives till the wedding."[124]

• When Wayne Gretzky was two years old, his father, Walter, started training him to be a hockey star. After buying the smallest hockey stick he could find, he cut it down even more so that Wayne could use it. He even built a hockey rink — complete with lights! — in the backyard so that Wayne could practice, even at night. The practice paid off. Mr. Gretzky became perhaps the greatest hockey player ever.[125]

• Comedian Tim Conway's father pretended that he had very sharp vision. Occasionally while driving, he would say, "Wasn't that a dime back there?" Then he would stop the car, and he and little Tim would get out, and sure enough, they would find a dime on the street. Not until he was an adult did Tim realize that his father had planted the dime on the street earlier just so he could "see" it later.[126]

• The artist Bela Haas was wealthy, but tight with his money. Once a well-dressed man asked him for some money, saying that he knew that Mr. Haas was rich, but Mr. Haas replied, "My dear sir, I am indeed rich, but I'm not generous and I must tell you that as my money is the only thing I have to remember my late-lamented father by, I can never part with it."[127]

• While Groucho Marx's son, Arthur, was in the Navy, Groucho visited him. Arthur helped him with the luggage, and with both his hands filled with luggage, he suddenly saw an admiral, who obviously expected to be saluted. Groucho came to the rescue. He saluted the admiral, then pointed to Arthur and explained, "He pays me to do his saluting for him."[128]

• The father of Sid Fleischman, author of the McBroom comedy series of children's books, owned a taxicab. One day, he discovered that if he hit a pothole, the meter would jump ahead, thus increasing the fare the passenger had to pay. After making this discovery, he learned the location of every pothole in the city.[129]

• Jay Leno's father didn't understand the importance of major celebrities maintaining some form of privacy. Whenever he learned that someone was a big fan of Jay, he would give the fan Jay's private telephone number and say, "Call him up! He'd love to hear from you!"[130]

• When Frank DeCaro, Jr., was born, his father did what he was supposed to and stayed in the hospital waiting room. However, although Frank, Jr., was born at 8 a.m., his father didn't learn about it until five hours later because the physician forgot to tell him.[131]

• When artist Louise Bourgeois was growing up, her father had a bad temper. At family dinners, her father always had a stack of cheap saucers by his side. That way, if he ever got angry, he could break a saucer instead of yelling at one of his children.[132]

• The English can be reserved. After English contralto Kathleen Ferrier had made a major stir in the world of opera, Bruno Walter congratulated her elderly father on Ms. Ferrier's success. Old Mr. Ferrier replied, "Yes, Kath's not doing too badly."[133]

• When Groucho Marx got married for the third time, he sent his son this telegram: "If you've heard about this, please refund the price of this telegram. Love from us both."[134]

• When Jack Benny was young, his father gave him two gifts: a violin, in case he had any musical talent, and a monkey wrench, in case he didn't have any musical talent.[135]

• Isaac Newton's father was illiterate. When he made out a will leaving his property, Woolsthorpe Manor, to his wife, he signed the will with an X.[136]

Father's Day

• Scaredy Kate is the pet cat of children's book illustrator Dyanne DiSalvo-Ryan. One Father's Day, Scaredy Kate gave birth to five kittens by the athletic shoes sitting in a corner of Dyanne's husband's closet. They named the five Father's Day gifts Adidas, Converse, Etonic, Nike, and Reebok.[137]

Food

• When he was a child, the mother of young-adult book author Walter Dean Myers set up a tab for him at the local grocer's — whenever young Walter was hungry, he could buy food and she would pay for it later. Walter, however, used the tab to buy chocolate, and soon all the neighborhood children knew that he could get "free" chocolate at the grocer's. As you would expect, Walter ordered lots and lots of chocolate, and after his mother had spoken sharply to him and to the grocer, he didn't have a tab anymore.[138]

• Marilyn Hall's mother-in-law once gave a dinner party for which the main course was a whole poached salmon. She instructed her new, foreign maid to bring in the salmon at a certain time "with a little parsley in the mouth." The maid did as she was told, but the dinner guests were very surprised when she brought in the salmon — the maid had parsley in her mouth.[139]

• Penn Jillette of Penn and Teller is still close to his old high-school teacher, Beverly C. Lucey. She remembers Penn and his friends sitting in the cafeteria eating their lunches — on the floor. This freaked out the vice principal, who wanted the students to sit in regular chairs at regular tables. Therefore, he ordered them to stand up. They did. Then he ordered them, "Sit down!" They did — back on the floor.[140]

• Irwin Shaw's son was raised in Paris and so was very sophisticated. After his first day in kindergarten, his nurse took him to a restaurant and asked what he wanted to order. He replied, "I'll have a dozen oysters and a glass of white wine."[141]

Friends

• When children's picture book creator Ezra Jack Keats was taking classes at the Art Students League, his best friend, Martin Pope, was taking science classes in college. Often, they would meet and have long discussions. Mr. Keats would walk Mr. Pope home, but since their discussion wasn't finished, they would turn around and Mr. Pope would walk Mr. Keats home. Because their discussion still wasn't finished, they would turn around again. Finally, they would say goodbye midway between their homes.[142]

• A group of musical performers partied together, and guitarist Hermann Leeb said to composer Frank Martin, "What a pity that there isn't any music that we could all play together!" The next morning, Mr. Martin called all the friends and asked them to come to his home. He had stayed up and written a piece for his friends and him to play together. "Berceuse" was written for piano four-hands, played by Madeleine Lipatti and Mr. Martin; guitar, played by Mr. Leeb; and voice, sung by the tenor Hugues Cuenod.[143]

• Ernestine Schumann-Heink had a problem when she first met Maurice Grau of the Metropolitan Opera Company — she did not have clothing fine enough for such an important meeting with such an important man. Fortunately, Lillian Nordica came to the rescue and lent her a silk dress — with a train — that made the necessary statement: The person wearing this dress is a prima donna. Later, Ms. Schumann-Heink embarrassed Ms. Nordica by thanking her publicly for the loan.[144]

• Albert Einstein was a friend to the Curie family, including both Marie and her daughter, Irène Joliot-Curie. One day, Mr. Einstein and Ms. Joliot-Curie were talking about particle tracks, as Ms. Joliot-Curie's daughter, Hélène, drew near them. Soon, young Hélène showed Mr. Einstein the "particle tracks" she had drawn. Mr. Einstein looked at the drawing, then told Ms. Joliot-Curie, "If you don't watch out, she'll become a theoretical physicist!" Hélène did.[145]

• Tenors Richard Tucker and Luciano Pavarotti were friends. After a performance by Mr. Tucker, Mr. Pavarotti called to congratulate him, saying, "I just can't believe it. I had to call you. You're still the top tenor in the world — a phenomenon." Whenever Mr. Tucker left a dressing room that would next be occupied by Mr. Pavarotti, he used to write on the mirror this message: "*Buona fortuna.*"[146]

• Madame Giulietta Grisi once decided to commit suicide, so she ran to a river so she could drown herself. Fortunately, a friend followed her and convinced her not to drown herself — making the argument that she would be disheveled, muddy, and unglamorous when her body was fished out of the river.[147]

• Children's picture book creator Ezra Jack Keats never had children of his own, but that was OK because his friends had children. Often, he would ask a friend, "Can I come and see how children climb out of a pillowcase?" or "I'm going to the zoo — can I borrow a child?"[148]

• Stan Laurel always had a great respect for his friend Oliver Hardy's talents as a comedian. Whenever Mr. Laurel watched one of the great comedy team's movies, he laughed at Mr. Hardy's antics, not at his own.[149]

Chapter 4: From Gays and Lesbians to Mothers

Gays and Lesbians

• Some lesbians have unusual coming-out stories. One lesbian told her abusive stepfather that she was a lesbian, and he immediately told her to get out of the house or he would give her a beating worse than the ones he had previously given her. Her straight siblings decided to take advantage of the situation to also get out of an abusive home — her straight brother immediately told their abusive stepfather that he was gay and a month later her straight sister told him that she was a lesbian. The lesbian adds, "My stepdad started to catch on, though, when my mother told him she was a lesbertarian."[150]

• Lesbian comedian Kate Clinton has a niece named Grace. One day, Grace and a friend were playing together, and Grace's mother heard Grace say, "Let's pretend we're gay!" Her friend asked, "What's gay?" Grace explained, "It's when two girls get together, dance, and have fun." While watching the March on Washington in 1993, Grace asked her mother, "Now tell me again, Mom, why do ungay people not like Aunt Kate?"[151]

Gifts

• Moravian soprano Maria Jeritza believed in causing a commotion and being talked about. When Beverly Sills was a child vocalist, she sang at a party where she met Ms. Jeritza, who presented her with a gold toothpick, saying, "You must become a character. You must make people talk about you. After we have all eaten, you pick your teeth with this gold toothpick, and you'll see — everybody will be talking about you."[152]

• Diamond Jim Brady loved to eat. He once ate a box of chocolates that came from the small Boston firm of Page and Shaw. He loved the candy and ordered several hundred boxes for himself and as gifts for his friends. Unfortunately, the business was too small to handle such a large order. Therefore, Diamond Jim gave them an interest-free loan of $150,000 so they could expand their candy-making capacity.[153]

• In the late 19th century, when the Crown Prince of Germany was engaged to the Princess, they stayed at Balmoral, where they found some white heather while walking. After they were married, the Crown Prince again stayed at Balmoral, where he found some white heather in the same place they had last found it. Knowing how much the Princess liked white heather, the Crown Prince sent it to her.[154]

• Sara, the wife of world-famous tenor Richard Tucker, was proud of her husband. Once, a business associate was trying to come up with a good idea for a gift for Mr. Tucker, so he asked Sara if he should give him calling cards. Sara replied, "What does he need calling cards for? Everybody knows who Richard Tucker is."[155]

Grandparents

• When comedian Arte Johnson was growing up on a farm in Michigan, everyone canned their own vegetables. One day, his family was boiling the canning jars to sterilize them when someone noticed a mouse in a spill area under the stove. They immediately shouted for Grampa to come and take care of the mouse. Annoyed, he came running from the barn carrying a shotgun, then aimed at the mouse and fired. He missed the mouse, but he did manage to shatter every canning jar on top of the stove. According to Mr. Johnson, "The green beans exploded and were hanging from the ceiling like stalactites for weeks."[156]

• When Walter Slezak got a job acting in New York, his grandmother sent a note to the captain of the ship that would take him to America. The note said this: "My grandson is sailing on your ship to America. Please keep an eye on him and drive carefully." The note amused the captain. On one occasion, Mr. Slezak was playing cards at 3:30 a.m., so the captain sent his steward to tell him it was time to go to bed. On another occasion, the seas were rough, so the captain sent Mr. Slezak a note: "I *am* driving carefully."[157]

• Ruth Anderson was the council president of the Akron, Ohio, Covenant Community Church. One year, her four-year-old granddaughter visited her all the way from Massachusetts. Ms. Anderson took her granddaughter to church, although her granddaughter's parents were not regular church-attending people. The granddaughter was impressed by the experience and told her parents, "They have a place they go to here in Ohio. They call it church."[158]

• Poet Nikki Giovanni, author of "Ego-Tripping," believes in family, and she also believes in being prepared. She feels that grandmothers ought to know how to bake cookies and other goodies for children, and when she learned that she would soon be a grandmother, she learned how to bake.[159]

Husbands and Wives

• A couple of coincidences saved the lives of married dancers Marian Ladré and Illaria Obidenna Ladré. Because Mrs. Ladré couldn't get a visa, she stayed behind in Romania while her husband went on tour in South America. Mrs. Ladré couldn't get a visa because of a mistake made by her mother, who couldn't speak much Romanian. When the Romanian bureaucrat asked her where her daughter was born, she thought they were asking her where her daughter was staying, and so she answered the question incorrectly. Because of the mistake, the bureaucrat wouldn't give her daughter a visa. The mistake saved Mrs. Ladré's life. Later, she started hemorrhaging and needed medical care immediately. If she had been in the jungles of South America, she would not have received the medical care she needed. At the same time Mrs. Ladré fell ill, her husband was on a train in the jungles of Brazil, unable to sleep because of worrying about his wife. The axle under his train car started burning. Because Mr. Ladré was awake, he was able to have the train stopped before an accident occurred.[160]

• Texas actor Marco Perella has a lot of respect for Drew Barrymore, with whom he worked in a movie titled *Home Fries* — he played a bad guy to her good girl. After the filming of the movie was completed, a bouquet of flowers arrived at Mr. Perella's home with a note reading, "Thanks for a wonderful time. Love, Drew." Underneath the signature was a lipstick kiss. Of course, Mrs. Perella was very interested in this bouquet and note, although nothing unprofessional had ever occurred between her husband and Ms. Barrymore. Mr. Perella finally convinced his wife that Ms. Barrymore had no doubt sent flowers and notes to every actor involved in the movie, but he noticed when the movie came out that his wife watched — very carefully — the scenes between him and Ms. Barrymore.[161]

• Donna Kloker of Great Falls, Montana, had a match-making student in one of the junior high courses she taught. The boy tried to match Donna with a barber in a barbershop where the boy shined shoes, even giving the barber Donna's telephone number. (Unfortunately, she was busy on the night that the barber wanted to set up a date.) One day, when she took the class on a field trip to the police station, the barber was inside, paying a traffic ticket. The student yelled, "That's him! That's him!" Then he pointed to Donna and told the barber, "That's her!" A few days later, Donna visited the barbershop — with the excuse of wanting to talk to her student — and some time afterward she and the barber were married.[162]

• At a performance of *Tannhaeuser* at the Metropolitan Opera, the singer playing the part of the Shepherd Boy became ill, so the stage manager, Paul Schumann, asked his wife, Ernestine Schumann-Heink, to take over the part. However, when the Shepherd Boy was supposed to come on stage and sing, Ms. Schumann-Heink simply stuck her head above a stage rock and sang without showing more of herself. Later, when she was asked why she had done that, she explained, "The Shepherd's Boy costume calls for tights, and that husband of mine —

do you think he would let me step out before an audience and show my legs? Not he!"[163]

• Ashe King worked at a dance studio and taught ballet. One day, a woman called to ask about the required clothing for her husband, who was thinking of taking a beginners' class. Mr. King explained that her husband would need ballet slippers, ballet tights, and a dance belt. When the woman asked what a dance belt was, Mr. King answered that all male dancers wore one, as it served to keep everything from flopping around. The woman then responded, "I can assure you, my husband does not need one of those — he is too small!" (The woman's husband never showed up for dance class, probably because he was too embarrassed.)[164]

• One day, Jay Leno and his wife, Mavis, decided to get in their car and go out for pizza. On this particular day, a Gay Pride March was being held, and they drove into the midst of a confusing scene. A police officer motioned them forward, and since Jay thought the officer was trying to help him get through the confusion, he followed the officer's directions. However, the officer put him in the midst of the parade. Jay and his wife drove for five miles as part of the parade, and all along the route he kept hearing people say, "Hey, look! I didn't know Jay Leno was gay!" Mr. Leno's wife thought this was hilarious.[165]

• One cold night, children's book author Joanna Cole and her husband, Phil, put an electric blanket on their bed incorrectly — her controls made his part of the blanket warmer or cooler, while his controls made her part of the blanket warmer or cooler. Joanna was freezing, so she kept turning up the heat. Eventually, she had turned up the heat as high as it would go and her husband jumped out of bed because he was burning up — only then did they figure out what had happened. According to Ms. Cole, she and her husband are not quite as mixed up as her characters Big Goof and Little Goof.[166]

• Comedian Bob Newhart's first date with his future wife, Virginia "Ginny" Quinn, was inauspicious. Mr. Newhart wasn't hungry, so he ordered a drink at the restaurant and watched her as she ate. This made her so nervous that she spilled mayonnaise on her dress. Mr. Newhart then announced that they were going to visit Carl Reiner and his family — people whom Ginny had never met. Once again, Ginny was nervous and during the entire visit she used her purse to cover the mayonnaise stain. About their first date, Ginny says, "I could have killed Bob."[167]

• Ivan Jadan, the premier lyric tenor of the Bolshoi Opera from 1928-1941, sang at the wedding of Barbara Mitchell, a friend in the Virgin Islands. He sang "The Lord's Prayer" at the wedding, then he sang Russian and Ukrainian folk songs at the reception. He was quite a good singer. After listening to him for over an hour, Barbara knew that it was time for her and her husband to go on their honeymoon, but she asked her mother, "Do I really have to leave?" (A man who had heard Mr. Jadan sing once remarked, "He doesn't sing; he prays.")[168]

• When Mark Twain wanted to marry Olivia Langdon, the daughter of a wealthy family in Connecticut, her father asked him to provide character references. Mr. Twain gave him the names of some prominent men, including ministers, whom he had known in the West. Unfortunately, the men reported that Mr. Twain was "born to be hung" and would end up in a "drunkard's grave." Nevertheless, Mr. Langdon allowed Mr. Twain to marry his daughter, saying, "Take the girl. I know you better than they do."[169]

• The 18th-century eccentric Timothy Dexter, who lived in Newburyport, Massachusetts, wanted a street named after himself in the town. The town officials declined to do so, and even Mr. Dexter's wife thought that it was a bad idea. However, Mr. Dexter found a novel way to get revenge on his wife. He simply woke up one morning and started referring to her as "the ghost that was my wife." She continued to live with him from that year, 1795, until he died in 1806, but he denied her living presence for all those years.[170]

• When Albert Schweitzer met and fell in love with Helene Breslau, he had already formed a plan to go to Africa as a physician.

He knew that his plan would result in lots of hardship, and he told Helene that he was worried that the hardship would be too much for her. Helene replied, "I will take a training course in nursing, and then you won't be able to get along without me." That's exactly what happened. She did take the training course, and she went to Africa as Dr. Schweitzer's nurse and wife.[171]

• In his Answer Man column, film critic Roger Ebert answered a question by Matt Sandler about who was the world's most beautiful woman by saying that she was Indian actress Aishwarya Rai. In a later Answer Man column, a reader stated that Mr. Ebert should have answered the question by saying, "My wife." However, Mr. Ebert had a good reason for not answering the question that way: "Matt Sandler asked about women, not goddesses."[172]

• Stephen Wozniak is famous because he and Steven Jobs started Apple, Inc. together. Mr. Wozniak met his wife when she dialed a Dial-a-Polish-Joke phone line he had set up. He talked with her for a few minutes, then said, "I bet I can hang up faster than you." He won, but a few days later she called him again and they set up a date. To decide whether to marry her, he flipped a coin — and kept on flipping it until it said to marry her.[173]

• Some spouses are very accommodating. While illustrating his Caldecott Medal-winning children's book, *Jumanji*, Chris Van Allsburg used photographs and models, as well as drawing from his imagination. He needed to draw pictures of monkeys, but he couldn't find any photographs of monkeys in the exact poses he needed, so his wife posed for him and he drew the monkeys using her as the model.[174]

• Director William Wellman once allowed his wife to play a small role in one of his movies. She had seven words of dialogue to begin with, but in the editing room her part was cut down to only three words. After seeing the movie, his wife told him, "Bill, I've been married to you for 13 years, and do you know what I've gotten out of it? Five kids and three words of dialogue."[175]

• Tom Waits often collaborates with his wife, Kathleen Brennan. For example, they co-wrote the stage play and musical titled *Frank's Wild Years*. Asked in an interview for *Spin* whether the two had worked together, or worked separately and sent stuff back and forth, Mr. Waits joked, "We sent stuff back and forth — like dishes, books, frying pans, vases."[176]

• Babe Didrikson's husband, George Zaharias, fully supported her athletic endeavors. Whenever she was about to compete in an important tournament, he slept in a separate bedroom so his snoring wouldn't bother her. Apparently, it helped — Babe won a record 17 golf tournaments in a row. (By the way, her husband's nickname for her was "Romance.")[177]

• Tenor Richard Lewis danced in perfect rhythm, of course, but his steps when dancing a fox-trot or a waltz were his own original creation. A friend, Brenda Webb, once danced with him, then complained to his wife, Elizabeth, who laughed, adding that it had taken her years to get used to her husband's dance steps.[178]

• Eleanor Roosevelt was an extremely active first lady, flying around the country visiting schools, hospitals, government buildings, etc. One day, the first lady's secretary told President Franklin Roosevelt that the first lady was in a prison. President Roosevelt joked, "I'm not surprised — but what for?"[179]

• When Henry Koster, director of *Harvey*, married actress Peggy Moran, he asked her to give up acting but promised to include her in every movie he directed. How did he keep his promise yet keep his wife from acting? In each movie he directed, a certain piece of art — a bust of his wife — appears.[180]

• Neither Dr. Seuss nor his wife liked to cook, and so they nearly always ate in restaurants. One day, his mother visited, and she was shocked when she opened the refrigerator door and discovered nothing inside except a cookbook that she had given the happy couple at their wedding.[181]

• Some people look for love in the wrong places. Philosopher Richard Watson once knew a man who was looking for his perfect soulmate: a woman who was willing to sail around the world with him. Mr. Watson asked, "And you're looking in St. Louis, Missouri?"[182]

• One night, singer Nat King Cole's wife woke him because he was snoring and joked, "Gosh, honey, we're going to have to get twin beds." He said immediately, "There'll be no twin beds in here!" Mrs. Cole says, "I loved it when he said that."[183]

• Grant Wood, painter of *American Gothic*, was married briefly. Following a big quarrel, his wife left him. This didn't seem to bother Mr. Wood much. After she left their house, he merely mowed the lawn and said, "I'm a free man again."[184]

• Shimon Apisdorf finds saying "I love you" to his wife is very easy, but he regards that as a problem. Such important words should not be said lightly; instead, they should be said with the deepest emotion.[185]

Illness

• When he was a child growing up in Harlem, children's book author Walter Dean Myers used to dance in the streets for money, which he used to buy his favorite red-colored icy pops. One day, after he had danced and eaten, danced and eaten, for hours, he went home with a stomachache. His mother set him on the toilet, then rushed him to the hospital after seeing the red liquid that had come out of his body. At the hospital, they learned that the red liquid was not blood — it was red-colored liquid from the many, many icy pops young Walter had consumed that day.[186]

• When Alicia Alonso could not see out of her right eye, she went to a doctor. He examined her eyes, then told her that she was going to be blind. She would not believe him and had an unsuccessful operation. Shortly afterward, her other eye went blind. Again, she had an operation, and her doctors told her that she had to stay in bed —

motionless — for a year. Alicia did not want her young daughter to know that she — Alicia — was blind, and for a year, whenever her daughter was brought into her room, Alicia pretended that she could see her through the bandages.[187]

• Some happily married heterosexual men like to dress like women. One way to get the proper female frontal development is for the man to wear a mastectomy bra. Many wives have ordered a mastectomy bra and been treated so nicely by the sales staff over the telephone that they have been tempted to say, "Don't worry. I don't have breast cancer. My husband just likes to wear a bra."[188]

• When beautiful actress Ann Jillian got breast cancer and underwent a double mastectomy, she worried about what her husband, Andy Murcia, would think when he saw the scars where her breasts had been. She needn't have worried. He looked, then said, "So, you've had a mastectomy and I'm still here." He hugged her, then said, "I'm not only still here. I'm not going anywhere."[189]

Letters

• When Janet Taylor Lisle was a child, she thought that she detected evidence of fairies. For example, when she found berries dotting the terrace, she thought that fairies had left them. She believed so strongly that she started writing letters to the fairies — and the fairies wrote her back! Of course, a loved one actually wrote the letters, not fairies, but this remains a pleasant memory. This memory served as inspiration for her children's book *The Gold Dust Letters*.[190]

• Maurice Sendak's picture book *Where the Wild Things Are* has long been a favorite of children, many of whom long to go to this land of fantasy. Mr. Sendak once received a letter from a boy who asked him how much it cost to travel to where the wild things are — if it wasn't too expensive, he and his sister wanted to spend the summer there. Mr. Sendak says, "I did not answer that question, for I have no doubt that sooner or later they will find their way, free of charge."[191]

Mothers

• While running his dog sled team one day, using a wheeled cart instead of a sled because it was spring, children's book author Gary Paulsen came across a dead ruffled grouse and a nest of her eggs. He took the 14 eggs home and put them in the nest of a banty hen named Hawk. This simple action may have been a mistake, as it brought down what his wife called a "summer of terror" on the Paulsen household. The eggs hatched, and Hawk devoted her life to protecting her chicks. However, ruffled grouse can fly much further than banty hens, which meant that Hawk had to patrol a wide area to protect the young grouse. Hawk therefore sat on top of a woodpile and whenever the grouse were threatened — or Hawk thought they were threatened — she charged down the woodpile and attacked whatever she thought needed attacking. A fox once grabbed a chick and Hawk slammed into the fox so hard that spit flew from the fox's mouth as it let go of the chick. Unfortunately, Hawk attacked some things that didn't need to be attacked — such as Mr. Paulsen's wife, son, cat, and dog. On one occasion, his wife went to get some tomatoes from the garden, and when she returned, the tomatoes were smeared on her shirt — this despite the bicycle helmet she had worn for protection from the attack that she knew was coming. Smeared with tomatoes, she announced to her husband, "The Hawk strikes again." After the ruffled grouse grew up, Hawk calmed down — but the Paulsen pets were still very careful when they were near her.[192]

• Although singer Ray Charles became blind when he was a child, his mother was determined that he would be treated like sighted children. One day, young Ray deliberately did a poor job of mopping the floor because he figured that since he couldn't see, his mother would let him get away with it. She didn't. Instead, she made him scrub the floor on his hands and knees. Ray didn't let his blindness interfere with the things he wanted to do. As a teenager, he drove a car with his friends sitting beside him to tell him when he was going too far to the right or to the left; he also drove a motorcycle, riding behind a friend's motorcycle and following the sound of its exhaust. In addition, he practically invented soul music by combining blues and gospel.[193]

• During the mid-1950s, Mikie, the little son of Metropolitan Opera soprano Regina Resnik, learned to enjoy opera music after a brief time of telling his mother, "No more practicing! I don't like opera music!" Soon his favorite music included "Three Blind Mice," "Little Red Monkey," and the overture from *Carmen*. Ms. Resnik frequently sang on TV, and her family would gather in the living room to watch her. Mikie would shout, "That's Mommy! That's Mommy!" That is, unless she was wearing a black wig over her own blond hair for a role. Then little Mikie would look at her and say sadly, "That's not Mommy. It's a different lady."[194]

• Sir James M. Barrie, author of *Peter Pan*, helped make Kensington Gardens famous, and as a reward he was given a key so he could roam the gardens in solitude after other people had left. He was quite pleased to be able to do so, for after he had written about Kensington Gardens in his book *The Little White Bird*, mothers used to lie in wait for him so they could introduce him to their children in hopes that he would use them in a book. (Sir James also used to put his mother, thinly disguised, into every book he wrote. She would read the book, then tell her son, "I'm thinking I am in it again!")[195]

• At the start of the Depression, comedian Jack Oakie's mother got worried about her son's money, which was deposited in the Bank of Hollywood. She insisted that he take all of his money out of the bank. Being a good son, he obeyed. When a bank teller asked his mother why she wanted Mr. Oakie to withdraw his money, she replied, "No particular reason. I just have the feeling that this might be a good day to take all of Jack's money out of the bank." It was a good thing she had this feeling — the bank failed to open the very next business day.[196]

• Frequently, when comic writer Robert Benchley wanted a plausible excuse for not completing a piece of writing by his deadline, he asked his mother to send telegrams, supposedly sent by himself, saying that she was ill and he was staying with her. However, sometimes he didn't care if the excuse was plausible. Once, he asked his mother to send this telegram in his name: "SORRY I CANT ATTEND LUNCHEON TODAY BECAUSE I AM IN BOSTON STOP DONT KNOW WHY I AM IN BOSTON BUT IT MUST BE IMPORTANT BECAUSE HERE I AM."[197]

• While Tim Conway was appearing on TV in the sitcom *McHale's Navy*, his mother called him to say, "You know, one of the Schutt boys is leaving the hardware store. There's an opening. You know the other boys, so if you could apply for that job, it would probably be to your benefit." He asked if she wanted him to work in a hardware store instead of on TV. She replied, "Yes — because the hardware store is a much steadier job. At least you know where you're going to work in the morning and how long you're going to be there."[198]

• When ballet dancer George Zoritch's aged mother was in a nursing home, she called a friend and said, "I need you. Don't ask questions. Just come here right away." The friend did come, taking three buses in 98-degree heat. When he arrived, he found her sitting quietly on the side of her bed. He asked, "What is the problem? You sounded distraught on the telephone." Mr. Zoritch's mother answered, "I am working on a crossword puzzle, and I didn't know what this word means, so I can't fill in the squares."[199]

• After Harry Houdini's mother died in 1913, Mr. and Mrs. Arthur Conan Doyle attempted to allow her spirit to communicate with Houdini through "automatic writing," in which Mrs. Doyle would allow Houdini's mother's spirit to use her hand to write a message to her son. In fact, a message was written — but it was written in English, and Houdini's mother knew only Yiddish. However, this didn't bother Mr. Doyle when Houdini pointed it out. Mr. Doyle felt that Houdini's mother had learned English in Heaven.[200]

• When lesbian humorist Laura Jimenez left home to go to college, her mother went out and bought a number of novelty envelopes. For a while, Laura was receiving personal mail from her mother in envelopes stating that the senders were such entities as "Johnson and Johnson Venereal Disease Research Center, Test Results Enclosed" and "Los Angeles Breast Augmentation Clinic." One envelope even bore this legend: "New, Color Illustrated Satanic Ritual Guide Enclosed."[201]

• When James McNeill Whistler wanted to paint his mother, it took him a while to find the right pose for her. For a few days she stood, but when she asked to sit down for a rest, Mr. Whistler realized that his mother, who was in her sixties, was too old to stand and pose for hours. He put her in a chair and gave her a footstool for her feet — this turned out to be the right pose. His *Arrangement in Grey and Black: Portrait of the Painter's Mother* became his most famous painting.[202]

• In Jackson, Mississippi, Eudora Welty's mother got her a public library card when she was nine years old. The librarian — Mrs. Calloway — was strict, sometimes sending girls home to change their clothes if she thought they weren't dressed properly. Because of the librarian's strictness, Mrs. Welty let her know specially that 9-year-old Eudora was allowed to check out any book she wanted — whether it came from the children's section or the adults' section of the library.[203]

• As a youngster, Buddy Holley (later, he became known as "Holly" because of a typo on a contract he signed) and Bob Montgomery played country music as a duo. Buddy and Bob once played at a seventh-grade dance, where they dedicated a song to the teachers: "Too Old to Cut the Mustard." Buddy's mother was present, and she was embarrassed. Later, she said that she wished the duo had picked a different song to dedicate to the teachers.[204]

• Children's book author Patricia MacLachlan loved to read when she was a little girl. She and her mother would walk to the library, and young Patricia would read the books as they walked home. Because Patricia was busy reading, her mother would put her hand on Patricia's neck and guide her as they walked home. By the time they reached home, Patricia had read all the books and wanted to go to the library again.[205]

• One of movie critic Roger Ebert's friends once worked for a pest control company while attending college. One day, he crawled under a house, exterminating pests with a spray gun. When he had finished, he crawled out, dirty and covered with cobwebs. The woman of the house invited him to drink lemonade, and as he drank it, she told her son, "Study your lessons hard, Jimmy, or you'll end up like him."[206]

• Lots of mothers watched the children's show *Captain Kangaroo* with their children. One day, Bob Keeshan, who played Captain Kangaroo, was having a drink with a friend in Hollywood. No one recognized him because he wasn't wearing the Captain's grey wig, but a woman in the bar complained, "My kids are in college, and I still keep hearing Captain Kangaroo's voice!"[207]

• Joel Perry went through puberty at the same time his mother was going through menopause, which meant that they had some interesting arguments. Once, he got his mother so angry that she shouted at him, "You son of a bitch!" He laughed and pointed at her, then she started laughing, too.[208]

• When Betty Friedan sold her house, her daughter, Emily, took prospective buyers through the house. Arriving at the third floor, where Ms. Friedan did her writing, Emily would proudly tell the prospective buyers, "And this is where my mother wrote *The Feminine Mystique*."[209]

• After her first book, *The Joy Luck Club*, became a runaway success, author Amy Tan was asked what her mother thought of the book. Ms. Tan replied that her mother went into bookstores, looking for her book, and if she didn't see it, she scolded the bookstore employees.[210]

• When novelist Jackie Collins was raising the two daughters she had with Oscar Lerman, the first word she taught them was not "Mummy" (she was born in London), but "Anything." Why? She wanted them to learn that they could do anything.[211]

• Paul Gauguin's mother knew that her son could be abrasive. After she died on July 7, 1867, she advised in her will that he start a career "since he has made himself so disliked by all my friends that he will one day find himself alone."[212]

• Soprano Rita Hunter's mother was very proud of her. While Ms. Hunter was singing in *Gotterdammerung*, her mother turned to a friend and asked, "My God, did I really give birth to that!"[213]

Chapter 5: From Music to Weddings

Music

• Sometimes people hear song lyrics incorrectly. For example, singer-songwriter Tom Waits' wife, Kathleen Brennan, thought that the refrain of Creedence Clearwater Revival's song "Bad Moon Rising" went, "There's a bathroom on the right." (Actually, as you entered many of the clubs that Mr. Waits used to perform in, there was a bathroom on the right.)[214]

• Ritchie Valens became famous as a result of singing such hits as "La Bamba," but when he was young, his family had a difficult time financially after his father died. In January 1958, his mother was unable to make a $65 house payment, so 17-year-old Ritchie and his band staged a dance. By charging $1.25 per person and $2 per couple, they made $125.[215]

• Soprano Geraldine Farrar started singing in public at a very young age — she performed her first song for a church concert at age three. When she had finished singing, she went to the front of the platform and asked, to the delight of the audience, "Did I do it well, mamma?"[216]

• Aretha Franklin started singing in the church choir when she was eight years old, and she made her professional debut — singing solo at church — when she was twelve years old. For singing, she was paid $15, which she immediately spent on a pair of roller skates.[217]

• Soprano Angelica Catalani was married to M. de Vallebregue, a French captain who lacked knowledge of music. When his wife complained that the piano was too high, he ordered a carpenter to cut six inches off each leg of the piano.[218]

• Sam Cooke started out as a gospel singer, but then he started to record pop songs. He worried about doing this, but his father, a minister, told him, "Sam, the Lord gave you a voice to make people happy. ... Go ahead and sing."[219]

Names

• Mark Twain's real name was Samuel Langhorne Clemens. When he was a steamboat pilot on the Mississippi River, he liked the words that rivermen called when they measured 12 feet of water. This much water had a depth of two fathoms, so the rivermen called out, "Mark twain." The phrase meant, "Note (or mark) that there are two (or twain) fathoms of water." Since two fathoms of water was deep enough to be safe for the steamboat, the pilot could heave a sigh of relief. Mr. Twain once took his family for a trip on a steamboat, and he stood on the deck listening to the cries of "Mark twain" coming from the rivermen. His daughter Clara came up to him and said, "I have hunted all over the boat for you. Don't you know they are calling for you?"[220]

• As a young girl, ballet dancer Mary Ellen Moylan decided that she needed a new, more romantic name; therefore, she chose "Mimi" and would not answer if she were called by any other name. However, returning to her lessons at the School of American Ballet, she discovered that her new name caused the other students to laugh at her, so she again went by the name of Mary Ellen.[221]

• Bryon, nicknamed "Brynie," was the eldest of the Seven Little Foys, whose real last name was Fitzgerald. When he met John Fitzgerald Kennedy, the President told him, "You know, Brynie, all we Fitzgeralds are related." Bryon asked, "What about Ella?"[222]

• When Darci Kistler, a ballerina for the New York City Ballet, was growing up, her nickname was "Crash." The nickname was the result of her learning to ride a small motorcycle — a Honda Yamaha 80 — and crashing into a tree.[223]

Parents

• The parents of stand-up comedian Carrie Snow are supportive of her choice of careers. In fact, her mother tells her, "Please make it soon. I hate those award ceremonies where people look up to the sky and say,

'Mom, if you're watching ....'" Ms. Snow inherited her sense of humor from her parents, who once placed this ad in a Jewish newspaper: "Our movie star daughter is too busy to look for a husband, so we'll look for her." Her mother even showed up at a pre-arranged meeting spot, wearing a carnation.[224]

• Paul Draper tap danced to classical music. However, before he was famous he became stranded without money in the South of France. He wired his parents for money and received the reply, "You've sown wild oats for long enough. Will send fare. Come home. Undertake some respectable profession." Mr. Draper gladly accepted the money and came home, but he went right on tap dancing to classical music.[225]

• Following her gold-medal-winning performance in the 1972 Olympic Games in Munich, Germany, Soviet gymnast Olga Korbut toured the United States. Before she left home to go on tour, her parents gave her this advice: "Be careful, be first, be joyful."[226]

Passover

• Metropolitan Opera tenor Richard Tucker and his family strictly observed the Jewish holidays, even while traveling in areas where Jews were rare. While in a restaurant in a Western city during Passover, they asked for the unleavened bread called *matzos* — but the waitress brought them matches.[227]

Practical Jokes

• Children's book author Gary Paulsen owned a dog named Columbia that had a sense of humor. Mr. Paulsen's dogs have separate houses and are chained — the chains keep them separated so that they can't fight each other. Every other day or so, each dog gets a big bone with some meat on it. Columbia took his bone and pushed it very close to the area that belonged to a dog named Olaf. The bone was so close that Olaf could lunge at the bone and touch it, but the bone was not so close that Olaf could get the bone and chew it. Columbia watched Olaf try to get the bone for several minutes, and then, according to

Mr. Paulsen, Columbia laughed. The realization that a dog could plan a practical joke like that, carry it out, and get enjoyment from it made Mr. Paulsen realize that dogs and other animals are more intelligent than they are often given credit for, and he stopped killing animals, even those animals he had been using for food.[228]

• While in high school, Stephen Wozniak created a ticking device which he placed in a gym bag. The principal heard the device, thought it was a bomb, grabbed the gym bag and took it outside the school. (Don't do this. Stephen got in trouble because of his practical joke.)[229]

Problem-Solving

• After actors Antonio Banderas and Melanie Griffith became a couple, they were plagued by the paparazzi, who followed them constantly during a visit to Spain, even when the couple wanted to be alone. Therefore, Mr. Banderas struck a deal with the paparazzi — if they would allow him and Ms. Griffith to be alone on Tuesdays and Thursdays, they would agree to be photographed the other days of the week.[230]

• When four-year-old Ekaterina Gordeeva, the future winner of two Olympic gold medals in pairs skating with Sergei Grinkov, started skating, even the smallest skates were too big for her feet. Her mother and grandmother solved the problem of little Ekaterina's feet slipping out of her skating boots by knitting several pairs of socks for her to wear while skating.[231]

• When he was 13 years old, Steven Spielberg had a problem with a bully who tormented him. He solved the problem by inviting the bully to star in a film he was making of soldiers fighting the Nazis in World War II. During the filming of *Battle Squad*, the two boys became best friends.[232]

• Even when Aretha Franklin was a school child, she had exceptional musical ability. Whenever the class became too rowdy, her teacher would settle the students down by asking young Aretha to play the piano and sing for them.[233]

• Sometimes, adopted children can be annoyed by nosy questions such as this: "Is that your real brother?" Some adopted children use the answer, "He isn't fake!"[234]

Siblings

• While managing the Hotel Rand in New York City, Wilson Mizner created a few rules for residents to follow. They included, "No opium-smoking in the elevators," "Guests must carry out their own dead," and "No piano-playing before 5 p.m. as it may disturb the other guests." One day, Mr. Mizner and a friend were walking down the street where the Hotel Rand was located, and Mr. Mizner crossed to the other side of the street, advising his friend, "Never walk under the hotel's windows. The girls throwing keys down to their friends will knock your brains out." His brother Henry, a preacher, once stayed at the hotel, so Mr. Mizner went to an employment agency to hire several women and children to sit in the hotel lobby and look respectable.[235]

• When children's book author Tomie DePaola was in kindergarten, his mother got pregnant, and he let her know that he wanted a sister with a red ribbon in her hair, although his mother told him that he wouldn't know if he had a brother or a sister until the baby arrived. When the baby arrived, he had a sister. As his parents were bringing the baby home, his mother and father stopped by Woolworth's, where they bought a red ribbon and tied it in his baby sister's hair before showing her to him for the first time.[236]

• Buddy Ebsen is perhaps best known as Jed Clampett in the TV series *The Beverly Hillbillies*; however, he and Vilma Ebsen were a popular brother-and-sister dance team in the 1930s. Buddy was very protective of his sister. Whenever she left in a taxicab, she used to look back and see him writing down the license number of the taxi in a notebook.[237]

• As a boy, movie director Steven Spielberg played pranks on his younger sisters: Sue, Anne, and Nancy. He once locked them in a closet with a skeleton that had a light glowing in its eye socket. And he once cut off the head of Nancy's favorite doll, then put it on a platter of lettuce, surrounded it with tomato slices, and served it to her.[238]

Sons

• One night, children's book author/illustrator David McPhail stayed up very late creating an illustration in which the character Henry Bear plays music in the rain. Despite his hard work, he wasn't sure whether he had correctly drawn the rain, but he knew that if he stayed up any later and worked on the illustration, he could ruin it. Early the next morning, Tristan, his five-year-old son, woke him up. Tristan had the illustration in his hand, and he told his father, "Henry Bear playing music in the rain — it's good!"[239]

• Feminist Betty Friedan sometimes felt guilty when something she wanted to do for herself interfered with an activity that involved her children. For example, she once turned down a chance to take a class in writing for television so that she could attend her son's Cub Scout meetings. However, after a few months, her son asked her if he could stop going to the Cub Scout meetings because they were boring. After that, she felt less guilty about doing the things she wanted to do for herself.[240]

• While acting in Jules Massenet's *Don Quichotte*, Feodor Chaliapin saw Boris, his son, in the wings. Although the scene required Mr. Chaliapin to be on his knees, crying, he managed to wink at his son with the eye not facing the audience, and even to whisper his son's Russian name: "Borka, Borka."[241]

Sports

• As a 12-year-old competitive athlete, Dorothy Hamill usually went to bed at 7 p.m. in order to get up at 5 a.m. so she could practice. She was ashamed of her early bedtime and worried that her friends might find out and make fun of her. Therefore, she made her mother promise that if anyone called after 7 p.m., she would tell them that Dorothy was out. Once, she went to a school dance. For this special occasion, her curfew was extended by an hour. While at the dance, she waited for a boy whom she liked to arrive. He walked in at 8 p.m. — the same time her father walked in to take her home.[242]

• When Billie Jean King was growing up in Long Beach, California, a tennis pro named Clyde Walker started giving free lessons in the public parks to any children who showed up. Each day, he traveled to a different park to give a lesson, and he soon noticed that no matter which park he went to, Billie Jean was there to receive instruction. He asked, "What are you up to? I just worked with you yesterday." Billie Jean replied, "This is how I'm going to get better."[243]

• When she was a kid, Sarah Tueting, a gold-medal winner as a goaltender on the United States women's hockey team at the 1998 Nagano Olympic Games, watched a goaltender during a game, moving from one end of the arena to the other as the goaltender changed positions. Her parents thought she had a crush on the boy, but she was actually studying his goaltending moves.[244]

• Jackie Joyner-Kersee became an Olympic gold medalist through lots of rigorous practice and training. When she was young, her family built her a long-jump pit near their porch. To get sand for the pit, Jackie and her sisters went to a nearby playground, filled empty potato chip bags with sand, then carried the sand back home.[245]

Weddings

• At one of the marriages Edwin Porter performed as a preacher in Texas during the first half of the 20th century, the best man took the wedding ring out of his pocket, passed it to the groom, who passed it to Rev. Porter, who passed it back to the groom, who placed it on the bride's finger. The bride had been watching the proceedings with interest, and being proud of her first ring, said to all present, "I know it's pure gold, or it would a-wore out with all that passin'."[246]

• On Saturday, May 25, 1963, tenor Richard Lewis and Elizabeth Robertson were married. That afternoon, beginning at 5:45 p.m., he performed in *Fidelio* at Glyndebourne. A notable aspect of the performance was the Male Chorus, composed of prisoners who should have looked downtrodden, but who were looking happy and inebriated — the result of the champagne reception.[247]

• When comedian Bob Newhart married Virginia "Ginny" Quinn in 1963, she wasn't completely sure she was doing the right thing, even as she walked down the aisle of the church. In fact, she was shaking so much that her father whispered to her, "Sweetheart, I can still get you out of this." (Fortunately, the marriage turned out to be happy.)[248]

• Marie Curie, two-time winner of the Nobel Prize, was very practical. When she got married to her husband, Pierre, she did not buy a white wedding dress that could be worn only once. Instead, she wore a navy gray suit — she deliberately chose a color that would not show dirt — that she could wear in the laboratory later.[249]

• In Poway, California, Msgr. Charles Dollen helped a prospective groom and bride to fill out a prenuptial-questions form. One question asked, "Are you entering this marriage of your own free will?" The nervous groom-to-be hesitated for a very long time, until finally his fiancée told him, "Put down 'Yes.'"[250]

Appendix A: Bibliography

Abdul, Raoul. *Famous Black Entertainers of Today*. New York: Dodd, Mead & Company, 1974.

Albani, Emma. *Forty Years of Song*. New York: Arno Press. 1977.

Aldape, Virginia Totorica. *David, Donny, and Darren*. Minneapolis, MN: Lerner Publications Company, 1997.

Alderson, Brian. *Ezra Jack Keats: Artist and Picture-Book Maker*. Gretna, LA: Pelican Publishing Co., Inc., 1994.

Aller, Susan Bivin. *J.M. Barrie: The Magic Behind Peter Pan*. Minneapolis, MN: Lerner Publications Company, 1994.

Allison, Amy. *Antonio Banderas*. Philadelphia, PA: Chelsea House Publishers, 2001.

Anderson, Margaret J. *Isaac Newton: The Greatest Scientist of All Time*. Springfield, NJ: Enslow Publications, Inc., 1996.

Apisdorf, Shimon. *Passover Survival Kit*. Columbus, OH: Leviathan Press, 1994.

Atkinson, Margaret F. and May Hillman. *Dancers of the Ballet*. New York: Alfred A. Knopf, 1955.

Benchley, Nathaniel. *Robert Benchley*. New York: McGraw-Hill Book Company, Inc., 1955.

Berman, Avis. *James McNeill Whistler*. New York: Harry N. Abrams, Inc., 1993.

Billings, Henry and Melissa. *Eccentrics: 21 Stories of Unusual and Remarkable People*. Providence, RI: Jamestown Publishers, 1987.

Borns, Betsy. *Comic Lives: Inside the World of American Stand-Up Comedy*. New York: Simon and Schuster, Inc., 1987.

Breslin, Herbert H., editor. *The Tenors*. New York: Macmillan Publishing Co., Inc., 1974.

Bunting, Eve. *Once Upon a Time*. Katonah, NY: Richard C. Owen Publishers, Inc., 1995.

Burke, John. *Rogue's Progress: The Fabulous Adventures of Wilson Mizner*. New York: G.P. Putnam's Sons, 1975.

Byars, Betsy. *The Moon and I*. Englewood Cliffs, NJ: Julian Messner, 1991.

Carroll, Cath. *Tom Waits*. New York: Thunder's Mouth Press, 2000.

Chippendale, Lisa A. *Triumph of the Imagination: The Story of Writer J.K. Rowling*. Philadelphia, PA: Chelsea House Publishers, 2002.

Christy, Marian. *Marian Christy's Conversations: Famous Women Speak Out*. Cambridge, MA: Lumen Editions, 1998.

Claxton, William, photographer. *Laugh: Portraits of the Greatest Comedians and the Funny Stories They Tell Each Other*. Introduction by John Lithgow; conceived and produced by Andy Gould and Kathleen Bywater; text edited by Mike Thomas. New York: William Morrow, 1999.

Clinton, Kate. *Don't Get Me Started*. New York: Ballantine Books, 1998.

Clower, Jerry. *Ain't God Good!* Waco, TX: Word Books, Publisher, 1975.

Cole, Joanna. *On the Bus with Joanna Cole*. With Wendy Saul. Portsmouth, NH: Heinemann, 1996.

Cole, Maria. *Nat King Cole: An Intimate Biography*. New York: William Morrow and Company, Inc., 1971.

Cummings, Pat, compiler and editor. *Talking with Artists*. New York: Bradbury Press, 1992.

Cummings, Pat, compiler and editor. *Talking with Artists, Volume 2*. New York: Simon & Schuster Books for Young Readers, 1995.

Davidson, Scooter Toby, and Valerie Anthony. *Great Women in the Sport of Kings: America's Top Women Jockeys Tell Their Stories*. New York: Syracuse University Press, 1999.

DeCaro, Frank. *A Boy Named Phyllis*. New York: Viking, 1996.

dePaola, Tomie. *26 Fairmount Avenue*. New York: G.P. Putnam's Sons, 1999.

dePaola, Tomie. *Here We All Are*. New York: G.P. Putnam's Sons, 2000.

Dole, Bob. *Great Presidential Wit*. New York: Scribner, 2001.

Douglas, Nigel. *More Legendary Voices*. London: Andre Deutsch Limited, 1994.

Edelson, Edward. *Funny Men of the Movies*. New York: Pocket Books, 1976.

Farrar, Geraldine. *Geraldine Farrar: The Story of an American Singer*. Boston, MA, and New York: Houghton Mifflin Company, 1916.

Fine, Edith Hope. *Gary Paulsen: Author and Wilderness Adventurer*. Berkeley Heights, NJ: Enslow Publications, Inc., 2000.

Fleischman, Sid. *The Abracadabra Kid*. New York: Greenwillow Books, 1996.

Frank, Rusty E. *Tap! The Greatest Tap Dance Stars and Their Stories, 1900-1955*. New York: William Morrow and Company, Inc., 1990.

Fraser, Lindsey. *Conversations with J.K. Rowling*. New York: Scholastic, Inc., 2000.

Furman, Leah. *Jennifer Lopez*. Philadelphia, PA: Chelsea House Publishers, 2001.

Garrett, Leslie. *Notes from a Small Soprano*. London: Hodder and Stoughton, 2000.

Greenberg, Jan, and Sandra Jordan. *The Painter's Eye: Learning to Look at Contemporary American Art*. New York: Delacorte Press, 1991.

Greenberg, Jan, and Sandra Jordan. *Runaway Girl: The Artist Louise Bourgeois*. New York: Harry N. Abrams, Inc., 2003.

Greenfeld, Howard. *Paul Gauguin*. New York: Harry N. Abrams, Publisher, 1993.

Hall, Marilyn, and Rabbi Jerome Cutler. *The Celebrity Kosher Cookbook*. Los Angeles, CA: J.P. Tarcher, Inc., 1975.

Hamill, Dorothy. *On and Off the Ice*. With Elva Clairmont. New York: Alfred A. Knopf, Inc., 1983.

Harmon, Jim. *The Great Radio Comedians*. Garden City, NY: Doubleday and Company, Inc., 1970.

Hecht, Andrew. *Hollywood Merry-Go-Round*. New York: Grosset and Dunlap, Publishers, 1947.

Heiderstadt, Dorothy. *Painters of America*. New York: David McKay Company, Inc., 1970.

Henry, Sondra, and Emily Taitz. *Betty Friedan: Fighter for Women's Rights*. Hillside, NJ: Enslow Publications, Inc., 1990.

Heuman, William. *Famous Coaches*. New York: Dodd, Mead & Company, 1968.

Heylbut, Rose, and Aimé Gerber. *Backstage at the Opera*. New York: Thomas Y. Crowell Company, 1937.

Hill, Anne E. *Ekaterina Gordeeva*. Philadelphia, PA: Chelsea House Publishers, 1999.

Hill, Christine M. *Ten Terrific Authors for Teens*. Berkeley Heights, NJ: Enslow Publications, Inc., 2000.

Hudry, Francois. *Hugues Cuenod: With a Nimble Voice*. Translated by Albert Fuller. Hillsdale, NY: Pendragon Press, 1998.

Hunter, Rita. *Wait Till the Sun Shines, Nellie*. London: Hamish Hamilton, Ltd., 1986.

Hyman, Trina Schart. *Self-Portrait: Trina Schart Hyman*. Reading, MA: Addison Wesley Publishing Company, Inc., 1981.

Jacobs, Karen Folger. *The Story of a Young Gymnast: Tracee Talavera*. New York: Bantam Books, Inc., 1980.

Jacobs, Linda. *Olga Korbut: Tears and Triumph*. St. Paul, MN: EMI Corporation, 1974.

Jadan, Doris. *The Great Life of Ivan Jadan*. St. John, Virgin Islands: Caribbean Booksmiths, 1995.

Jimenez, Laura. *Hear Me OUT!: A Dose of Lesbian Humor for the Whole Human Race*. San Jose, New York, Lincoln, Shanghai: Writers Club Press, 2001.

Josephson, Judith Pinkerton. *Nikki Giovanni: Poet of the People*. Berkeley Heights, NJ: Enslow Publications, Inc., 2000.

Kistler, Darci. *Ballerina: My Story*. With Alicia Kistler. New York: Pocket Books, Inc., 1993.

Knapp, Ron. *American Legends of Rock*. Springfield, NJ: Enslow Publications, Inc., 1996.

Korman, Susan. *Christina Aguilera*. Philadelphia, PA: Chelsea House Publishers, 2001.

Kovacs, Deborah. *Meet the Authors*. New York: Scholastic Professional Books, 1995.

Kovacs, Deborah, and James Preller. *Meet the Authors and Illustrators*. New York: Scholastic, Inc., 1991.

Kramer, Barbara. *Amy Tan: Author of* The Joy Luck Club. Springfield, NJ: Enslow Publications, Inc., 1996.

Ladré, Illaria Obidenna. *Illaria Obidenna Ladré: Memoirs of a Child of Theatre Street*. With Nancy Whyte. Seattle, WA: The Author, 1988.

Lahee, Henry C. *Famous Singers of To-day and Yesterday*. Boston, MA: L.C. Page and Company, 1898.

Leder, Jane Mersky. *Wayne Gretzky*. Mankato, MN: Crestwood House, Inc., 1985.

Leipold, L. Edmond. *Famous American Artists*. Minneapolis, MN: T.S. Denison and Company, Inc., 1969.

Leno, Jay. *Leading With My Chin*. With Bill Zehme. New York: HarperCollins Publishers, Inc., 1996.

Lester, Julius. *The Blues Singers: Ten Who Rocked the World*. New York: Hyperion Books for Children, 2001.

Littlefield, Bill. *Champions: Stories of Ten Remarkable Athletes*. Boston, MA: Little, Brown and Company, 1993.

Lowry, Lois. *Looking Back: A Book of Memories*. Boston: Houghton Mifflin Company, 1998.

Macy, Sue. *A Whole New Ball Game: The Story of the All-American Girls Professional Baseball League*. New York: Henry Holt and Company, 1993.

Marcus, Leonard S., compiler and editor. *Author Talk*. New York: Simon and Schuster Books for Young Readers, 2000.

Marcus, Leonard S. *A Caldecott Celebration: Six Artists and Their Paths to the Caldecott Medal*. New York: Walker and Company, 1998.

Marx, Arthur. *Son of Groucho*. New York: David McKay Company, Inc., 1972.

Matz, Mary Jane. *Opera Stars in the Sun: Intimate Glimpses of Metropolitan Personalities*. New York: Farrar, Straus, and Cudahy, 1955.

McKown, Robin. *The World of Mary Cassatt*. New York: Dell Publishing Co., Inc., 1972.

McPhail, David. *In Flight with David McPhail*. Katonah, NY: Richard C. Owen Publishers, Inc., 1996.

Mercredi, Morningstar. *Fort Chipewyan Homecoming: A Journey to Native Canada*. Minneapolis, MN: Lerner Publications Company, 1997.

Mingo, Jack. *The Juicy Parts*. New York: The Berkley Publishing Group, 1996.

Mostel, Kate, and Madeline Gilford. *170 Years of Show Business*. With Jack Gilford and Zero Mostel. New York: Random House, 1978.

Mott, Robert L. *Radio Live! Television Live!: Those Golden Days When Horses Were Coconuts*. Jefferson, NC: McFarland & Company, Inc., Publishers, 2000.

Myers, Walter Dean. *Bad Boy: A Memoir*. New York: HarperCollins Publishers, 2001.

Northrup, Mary. *American Computer Pioneers*. Springfield, NJ: Enslow Publications, Inc., 1998.

Oakie, Victoria Horne, compiler and editor. *"Dear Jack": Hollywood Birthday Reminiscences to Jack Oakie*. Portland, OR: Strawberry Hill Press, 1994.

Orleans, Ellen. *The Inflatable Butch*. Los Angeles, CA: Alyson Books, 2001.

Paulsen, Gary. *Woodsong*. New York: Bradbury Press, 1990.

Pegg, Robert. *Comical Co-Stars of Television*. Jefferson, NC: McFarland & Company, Inc., Publishers, 2002.

Perella, Marco. *Adventures of a No Name Actor*. New York: Bloomsbury, 2002.

Perry, Joel. *Funny That Way: Adventures in Fabulousness*. Los Angeles, CA: Alyson Books, 2001.

Pflaum, Rosalynd. *Marie Curie and Her Daughter Irene*. Minneapolis, MN: Lerner Publications Company, 1993.

Pflueger, Lynda. *Mark Twain: Legendary Writer and Humorist*. Berkeley Heights, NJ: Enslow Publications, Inc., 1999.

Porter, Alyene. *Papa was a Preacher*. New York: Abingdon Press, 1944.

Powers, Tom. *Steven Spielberg: Master Storyteller*. Minneapolis, MN: Lerner Publications Company, 1997.

Rappoport, Ken, and Barry Wilner. *Girls Rule! The Glory and Spirit of Women in Sports*. Kansas City, MO: Andrews McMeel Publishing, 2000.

Ravitch, Diane, editor. *The American Reader: Words That Moved a Nation*. New York: HarperCollins Publishers, 1990.

Rayner, William P. *Wise Women*. New York: St. Martin's Press, 1983.

Rediger, Pat. *Great African Americans in Sports*. New York: Crabtree Publishing Company, 1996.

Rosen, Michael J., editor. *Purr ... Children's Book Illustrators Brag About Their Cats*. San Diego, CA: Harcourt Brace and Company, 1996.

Rosen, Michael J., editor. *Speak! Children's Book Illustrators Brag About Their Dogs*. San Diego, CA: Harcourt Brace and Company, 1993.

Ross-Russell, Noel. *There Will I Sing*. London: Open Gate Press, 1996.

Russell, Anna. *I'm Not Making This Up, You Know: The Autobiography of the Queen of Musical Parody*. New York: The Continuum Publishing Company, 1985.

Samra, Cal and Rose, editors. *Holy Hilarity*. Colorado Springs, CO: WaterBrook Press, 1999.

Samra, Cal and Rose, editors. *More Holy Humor*. Colorado Springs, CO: WaterBrook Press, 1997.

Schwartz, Perry. *Carolyn's Story*. Minneapolis, MN: Lerner Publications Company, 1996.

Scott, Kieran. *Cameron Diaz*. Philadelphia, PA: Chelsea House Publishers, 2001.

Seroff, Victor. *Renata Tebaldi: The Woman and the Diva*. Freeport, NY: Books for Libraries Press, 1970.

Sheafer, Silvia Anne. *Aretha Franklin: Motown Superstar*. Springfield, NJ: Enslow Publications, Inc., 1996.

Slezak, Leo. *Song of Motley*. New York: Arno Press, 1977.

Slezak, Walter. *What Time's the Next Swan?* Garden City, NY: Doubleday and Co., Inc., 1962.

Smaridge, Norah. *Famous Author-Illustrators for Young People*. New York: Dodd, Mead & Company, 1973.

Smith, H. Allen. *Life in a Putty Knife Factory*. Philadelphia, PA: The Blakiston Company, 1943.

Sorensen, Jeff. *Bob Newhart*. New York: St. Martin's Press, 1988.

Spinelli, Jerry. *Knots in My Yo-yo String: The Autobiography of a Kid*. New York: Alfred A. Knopf, 1998.

Stevens, William Oliver. *Famous Humanitarians*. New York: Dodd, Mead & Company, 1953.

Stier, Theodore. *With Pavlova Around the World*. London: Hurst & Blackett, Ltd., 1927.

Stone, Laurie. *Laughing in the Dark: A Decade of Subversive Comedy*. Hopewell, NJ: The Ecco Press, 1997.

Strudwick, Leslie. *Athletes*. New York: Crabtree Publishing Company, 1999.

Tevis, Jamie Griggs. *My Life with the Hustler*. Athens, OH: The Author, 2003.

Van Dyke, Dick. *Those Funny Kids!* Garden City, NY: Doubleday and Company, Inc., 1975.

Vera, Veronica. *Miss Vera's Cross-Dress for Success*. New York: Villard Books, 2002.

Verde, Tom. *Twentieth-Century Writers: 1950-1990*. New York: Facts on File, Inc., 1996.

Watson, Richard A. *Good Teaching*. Carbondale, IL: Southern Illinois University Press, 1997.

Watson, Richard. *The Philosopher's Diet: How to Lose Weight and Change the World*. Boston, MA: The Atlantic Monthly Press, 1985.

Weidt, Maryann N. *Oh, the Places He Went: A Story About Dr. Seuss*. Minneapolis, MN: Carolrhoda Books, Inc., 1994.

Zoritch, George. *Ballet Mystique: Behind the Glamour of the Ballet Russe*. Mountain View, CA: Cynara Editions, 2000.

Appendix B: About the Author

It was a dark and stormy night. Suddenly a cry rang out, and on a hot summer night in 1954, Josephine, wife of Carl Bruce, gave birth to a boy — me. Unfortunately, this young married couple allowed Reuben Saturday, Josephine's brother, to name their first-born. Reuben, aka "The Joker," decided that Bruce was a nice name, so he decided to name me Bruce Bruce. I have gone by my middle name — David — ever since.

Being named Bruce David Bruce hasn't been all bad. Bank tellers remember me very quickly, so I don't often have to show an ID. It can be fun in charades, also. When I was a counselor as a teenager at Camp Echoing Hills in Warsaw, Ohio, a fellow counselor gave the signs for "sounds like" and "two words," then she pointed to a bruise on her leg twice. Bruise Bruise? Oh yeah, Bruce Bruce is the answer!

Uncle Reuben, by the way, gave me a haircut when I was in kindergarten. He cut my hair short and shaved a small bald spot on the back of my head. My mother wouldn't let me go to school until the bald spot grew out again.

Of all my brothers and sisters (six in all), I am the only transplant to Athens, Ohio. I was born in Newark, Ohio, and have lived all around Southeastern Ohio. However, I moved to Athens to go to Ohio University and have never left.

At OU, I never could make up my mind whether to major in English or Philosophy, so I got a bachelor's degree with a double major in both areas in 1980, then I added a master's degree in English in 1984 and a master's degree in Philosophy in 1985. Currently, and for a long time to come, I publish a weekly humorous column titled "Wise Up!" for *The Athens NEWS* and I am an English instructor at OU.

If all goes well, I will publish one or two books a year for the rest of my life. (On the other hand, a good way to make God laugh is to tell Her your plans.

By the way, my sister Brenda Kennedy writes romances such as *A New Beginning* and *Shattered Dreams*.

Appendix C: Some Books by David Bruce

Anecdote Collections

250 Anecdotes About Opera
250 Anecdotes About Religion
250 Anecdotes About Religion: Volume 2
250 Music Anecdotes
Be a Work of Art: 250 Anecdotes and Stories
The Coolest People in Art: 250 Anecdotes
The Coolest People in the Arts: 250 Anecdotes
The Coolest People in Books: 250 Anecdotes
The Coolest People in Comedy: 250 Anecdotes
Create, Then Take a Break: 250 Anecdotes
Don't Fear the Reaper: 250 Anecdotes
The Funniest People in Art: 250 Anecdotes
The Funniest People in Books: 250 Anecdotes
The Funniest People in Books, Volume 2: 250 Anecdotes
The Funniest People in Books, Volume 3: 250 Anecdotes
The Funniest People in Comedy: 250 Anecdotes
The Funniest People in Dance: 250 Anecdotes
The Funniest People in Families: 250 Anecdotes
The Funniest People in Families, Volume 2: 250 Anecdotes
The Funniest People in Families, Volume 3: 250 Anecdotes
The Funniest People in Families, Volume 4: 250 Anecdotes
The Funniest People in Families, Volume 5: 250 Anecdotes
The Funniest People in Families, Volume 6: 250 Anecdotes
The Funniest People in Movies: 250 Anecdotes
The Funniest People in Music: 250 Anecdotes
The Funniest People in Music, Volume 2: 250 Anecdotes
The Funniest People in Music, Volume 3: 250 Anecdotes
The Funniest People in Neighborhoods: 250 Anecdotes
The Funniest People in Relationships: 250 Anecdotes
The Funniest People in Sports: 250 Anecdotes
The Funniest People in Sports, Volume 2: 250 Anecdotes
The Funniest People in Television and Radio: 250 Anecdotes
The Funniest People in Theater: 250 Anecdotes

The Funniest People Who Live Life: 250 Anecdotes
The Funniest People Who Live Life, Volume 2: 250 Anecdotes
The Kindest People Who Do Good Deeds, Volume 1: 250 Anecdotes
The Kindest People Who Do Good Deeds, Volume 2: 250 Anecdotes
Maximum Cool: 250 Anecdotes
The Most Interesting People in Movies: 250 Anecdotes
The Most Interesting People in Politics and History: 250 Anecdotes
The Most Interesting People in Politics and History, Volume 2: 250 Anecdotes
The Most Interesting People in Politics and History, Volume 3: 250 Anecdotes
The Most Interesting People in Religion: 250 Anecdotes
The Most Interesting People in Sports: 250 Anecdotes
The Most Interesting People Who Live Life: 250 Anecdotes
The Most Interesting People Who Live Life, Volume 2: 250 Anecdotes
Reality is Fabulous: 250 Anecdotes and Stories
Resist Psychic Death: 250 Anecdotes
Seize the Day: 250 Anecdotes and Stories

[1] Source: William P. Rayner, *Wise Women*, p. 199.

[2] Source: Judith Pinkerton Josephson, *Nikki Giovanni: Poet of the People*, p. 31.

[3] Source: Edith Hope Fine, *Gary Paulsen: Author and Wilderness Adventurer*, pp. 53-55, 82, 84.

[4] Source: Betsy Byars, *The Moon and I*, pp. 8-10.

[5] Source: Michael J. Rosen, editor, *Purr ... Children's Book Illustrators Brag About Their Cats*, p. 12.

[6] Source: Veronica Vera, *Miss Vera's Cross-Dress for Success*, p. 37.

[7] Source: Scooter Toby Davidson and Valerie Anthony, *Great Women in the Sport of Kings: America's Top Women Jockeys Tell Their Stories*, pp. 27-29.

[8] Source: Theodore Stier, *With Pavlova Around the World*, pp. 129-130.

[9] Source: Tom Verde, *Twentieth-Century Writers: 1950-1990*, pp. 128-129, 130, 139.

[10] Source: Emma Albani, *Forty Years of Song*, pp. 136-137.

[11] Source: Virginia Totorica Aldape, *David, Donny, and Darren*, p. 14.

[12] Source: Michael J. Rosen, editor, *Speak! Children's Book Illustrators Brag About Their Dogs*, p. 2.

[13] Source: Maryann N. Weidt, *Oh, the Places He Went: A Story About Dr. Seuss*, p. 50.

[14] Source: Pat Cummings, compiler and editor, *Talking with Artists, Volume 2*, p. 61.

[15] Source: Jan Greenberg and Sandra Jordan, *The Painter's Eye*, pp. 10-11.

[16] Source: Howard Greenfeld, *Paul Gauguin*, p. 48.

[17] Source: Marco Perella, *Adventures of a No Name Actor*, pp. 125-127.

[18] Source: Rita Hunter, *Wait Till the Sun Shines, Nellie*, p. 93.

[19] Source: Lois Lowry, *Looking Back: A Book of Memories*, pp. 59-60.

[20] Source: Sue Macy, *A Whole New Ball Game: The Story of the All-American Girls Professional Baseball League*, p. xvi.

[21] Source: Maria Cole, *Nat King Cole: An Intimate Biography*, pp. 96-97.

[22] Source: Sue Macy, *A Whole New Ball Game: The Story of the All-American Girls Professional Baseball League*, p. 22.

[23] Source: William Heuman, *Famous Coaches*, p. 88.

[24] Source: Ken Rappoport and Barry Wilner, *Girls Rule!*, p. 39.

[25] Source: William P. Rayner, *Wise Women*, p. 239.

[26] Source: Avis Berman, *James McNeill Whistler*, pp. 7, 9, 11.

[27] Source: Jerry Clower, *Ain't God Good!*, p. 30.

[28] Source: Tomie dePaola, *26 Fairmount Avenue*, pp. 9-15.

[29] Source: Susan Korman, *Christina Aguilera*, pp. 22-23, 31-32, 52-53.

[30] Source: Morningstar Mercredi, *Fort Chipewyan Homecoming: A Journey to Native Canada*, pp. 8-9.

[31] Source: Karen Folger Jacobs, *The Story of a Young Gymnast: Tracee Talavera*, pp. 1, 4.

[32] Source: Deborah Kovacs and James Preller, *Meet the Authors and Illustrators*, pp. 38-39.

[33] Source: Trina Schart Hyman, *Self-Portrait: Trina Schart Hyman*, the section titled "Little Red Riding Hood." (The pages of this short children's book are unnumbered.)

[34] Source: Eve Bunting, *Once Upon a Time*, pp. 16-18.

[35] Source: Tomie dePaola, *Here We All Are*, p. 5.

[36] Source: Walter Slezak, *What Time's the Next Swan?*, p. 12.

[37] Source: L. Edmond Leipold, *Famous American Artists*, p. 22.

[38] Source: Leslie Strudwick, *Athletes*, pp. 6-7.

[39] Source: Christine M. Hill, *Ten Terrific Authors for Teens*, p. 93.

[40] Source: Frank DeCaro, *A Boy Named Phyllis*, pp. 45-46.

[41] Source: Robin McKown, *The World of Mary Cassatt*, p. 126.

[42] Source: Scooter Toby Davidson and Valerie Anthony, *Great Women in the Sport of Kings: America's Top Women Jockeys Tell Their Stories*, p. 13.

[43] Source: Jamie Griggs Tevis, *My Life with the Hustler*, pp. 47, 49.

[44] Source: Jerry Spinelli, *Knots in My Yo-yo String: The Autobiography of a Kid*, p. 62.

[45] Source: Joanna Cole, *On the Bus with Joanna Cole*, pp. 36-37.

[46] Source: Bill Littlefield, *Champions: Stories of Ten Remarkable Athletes*, p. 70.

[47] Source: Dick Van Dyke, *Those Funny Kids!*, pp. 45-46.

[48] Source: Geraldine Farrar, *Geraldine Farrar: The Story of an American Singer*, pp. 12-13.

[49] Source: Eve Bunting, *Once Upon a Time*, pp. 5-6.

[50] Source: Leonard S. Marcus, compiler and editor, *Author Talk*, pp. 50-51.

[51] Source: Sid Fleischman, *The Abracadabra Kid*, p. 65.

[52] Source: Edith Hope Fine, *Gary Paulsen: Author and Wilderness Adventurer*, p. 85.

[53] Source: Pat Cummings, compiler and editor, *Talking with Artists*, p. 16.

[54] Source: L. Edmond Leipold, *Famous American Artists*, p. 21.

[55] Source: Raoul Abdul, *Famous Black Entertainers of Today*, pp. 146-147.

[56] Source: H. Allen Smith, *Life in a Putty Knife Factory*, p. 51.

[57] Source: Norah Smaridge, *Famous Author-Illustrators for Young People*, p. 115.

[58] Source: Perry Schwartz, *Carolyn's Story*, p. 17.

[59] Source: David McPhail, *In Flight with David McPhail*, p. 2.

[60] Source: Pat Cummings, compiler and editor, *Talking with Artists*, p. 67.

[61] Source: Susan Bivin Aller, *J.M. Barrie: The Magic Behind Peter Pan*, p. 42.

[62] Source: Robin McKown, *The World of Mary Cassatt*, p. 109.

[63] Source: Cal and Rose Samra, *Holy Hilarity*, p. 27.

[64] Source: Edward Edelson, *Funny Men of the Movies*, p. 29.

[65] Source: Jim Harmon, *The Great Radio Comedians*, p. 94.

[66] Source: Lindsey Fraser, *Conversations with J.K. Rowling*, pp. 32-33.

[67] Source: Barbara Kramer, *Amy Tan: Author of* The Joy Luck Club, p. 8.

[68] Source: Lisa A. Chippendale, *Triumph of the Imagination: The Story of Writer J.K. Rowling*, p. 22.

[69] Source: Jamie Griggs Tevis, *My Life with the Hustler*, p. 115.

[70] Source: Walter Slezak, *What Time's the Next Swan?*, p. 17.

[71] Source: Dorothy Heiderstadt, *Painters of America*, p. 97.

[72] Source: Bob Dole, *Great Presidential Wit*, p. 56.

[73] Source: Dorothy Hamill, *On and Off the Ice*, p. 13.

[74] Source: Pat Cummings, compiler and editor, *Talking with Artists, Volume 2*, p. 25.

[75] Source: Virginia Totorica Aldape, *David, Donny, and Darren*, p. 11.

[76] Source: Kate Mostel and Madeline Gilford, *170 Years of Show Business*, p. 80.

[77] Source: Trina Schart Hyman, *Self-Portrait: Trina Schart Hyman*, the section titled "Kloraine and Lacey." (The pages of this short children's book are unnumbered.)

[78] Source: Ellen Orleans, *The Inflatable Butch*, pp. 107-110.

[79] Source: Alyene Porter, *Papa was a Preacher*, pp. 145-146.

[80] Source: Robert L. Mott, *Radio Live! Television Live!*, pp. 62-63.

[81] Source: Leonard S. Marcus, compiler and editor, *Author Talk*, p. 50.

[82] Source: Doris Jadan, *The Great Life of Ivan Jadan*, pp. 17-18.

[83] Source: Jan Greenberg and Sandra Jordan, *Runaway Girl: The Artist Louise Bourgeois*, p. 8.

[84] Source: Margaret J. Anderson, *Isaac Newton: The Greatest Scientist of All Time*, pp. 5, 7.

[85] Source: Betsy Borns, *Comic Lives*, pp. 124-125.

[86] Source: William Claxton, *Laugh*, p. 24.

[87] Source: Amy Allison, *Antonio Banderas*, p. 13.

[88] Source: Darci Kistler, *Ballerina: My Story*, p. 104.

[89] Source: Laurie Stone, *Laughing in the Dark*, p. 196.

[90] Source: Lisa A. Chippendale, *Triumph of the Imagination: The Story of Writer J.K. Rowling*, p. 72.

[91] Source: Laurie Stone, *Laughing in the Dark*, pp. 50-51.

[92] Source: Victor Seroff, *Renata Tebaldi: The Woman and the Diva*, p. 164.

[93] Source: Nathaniel Benchley, *Robert Benchley*, pp. 15-16, 35-36.

[94] Source: Leslie Garrett, *Notes from a Small Soprano*, p. 228.

[95] Source: Laura Jimenez, *Hear Me OUT!: A Dose of Lesbian Humor for the Whole Human Race*, p. 111.

[96] Source: Anne E. Hill, *Ekaterina Gordeeva*, p. 82.

[97] Source: John Burke, *Rogue's Progress: The Fabulous Adventures of Wilson Mizner*, p. 277.

[98] Source: Michael J. Rosen, editor, *Speak! Children's Book Illustrators Brag About Their Dogs*, p. 11.

[99] Source: Betsy Byars, *The Moon and I*, pp. 70-72.

[100] Source: Jan Greenberg and Sandra Jordan, *The Painter's Eye*, pp. 68-69.

[101] Source: Linda Jacobs, *Olga Korbut: Tears and Triumph*, pp. 37-38.

[102] Source: Tomie dePaola, *26 Fairmount Avenue*, pp. 32-37.

[103] Source: Karen Folger Jacobs, *The Story of a Young Gymnast: Tracee Talavera*, p. 38.

[104] Source: Leslie Garrett, *Notes from a Small Soprano*, pp. 18-19.

[105] Source: Richard A. Watson, *Good Teaching*, p. 35.

[106] Source: Deborah Kovacs, *Meet the Authors*, p. 83.

[107] Source: Richard A. Watson, *Good Teaching*, pp. 41-42.

[108] Source: Christine M. Hill, *Ten Terrific Authors for Teens*, p. 51.

[109] Source: Cal and Rose Samra, editors, *More Holy Humor*, p. 49.

[110] Source: Jerry Spinelli, *Knots in My Yo-yo String: The Autobiography of a Kid*, p. 19.

[111] Source: Leah Furman, *Jennifer Lopez*, p. 22.

[112] Source: Lindsey Fraser, *Conversations with J.K. Rowling*, p. 17.

[113] Source: Mary Northrup, *American Computer Pioneers*, pp. 67-68.

[114] Source: William Oliver Stevens, *Famous Humanitarians*, p. 15.

[115] Source: Lois Lowry, *Looking Back: A Book of Memories*, pp. 79-81.

[116] Source: Kieran Scott, *Cameron Diaz*, pp. 16-17.

[117] Source: Anna Russell, *I'm Not Making This Up, You Know*, p. 82.

[118] Source: William Claxton, *Laugh*, p. 58.

[119] Source: Diane Ravitch, editor, *The American Reader*, p. 89.

[120] Source: Kate Clinton, *Don't Get Me Started*, p. 15.

[121] Source: H. Allen Smith, *Life in a Putty Knife Factory*, p. 19.

[122] Source: Silvia Anne Sheafer, *Aretha Franklin: Motown Superstar*, p. 43.

[123] Source: Pat Rediger, *Great African Americans in Sports*, p. 52.

[124] Source: William Heuman, *Famous Coaches*, p. 93.

[125] Source: Jane Mersky Leder, *Wayne Gretzky*, p. 6.

[126] Source: Robert Pegg, *Comical Co-Stars of Television*, p. 54.

[127] Source: Leo Slezak, *Song of Motley*, p. 293.

[128] Source: Arthur Marx, *Son of Groucho*, p. 217.

[129] Source: Sid Fleischman, *The Abracadabra Kid*, p. 12.

[130] Source: Jay Leno, *Leading With My Chin*, p. 257.

[131] Source: Frank DeCaro, *A Boy Named Phyllis*, p. 2.

[132] Source: Jan Greenberg and Sandra Jordan, *Runaway Girl: The Artist Louise Bourgeois*, p. 15.

[133] Source: Nigel Douglas, *More Legendary Voices*, p. 74.

[134] Source: Arthur Marx, *Son of Groucho*, p. 289.

[135] Source: Jim Harmon, *The Great Radio Comedians*, p. 155.

[136] Source: Margaret J. Anderson, *Isaac Newton: The Greatest Scientist of All Time*, p. 14.

[137] Source: Michael J. Rosen, editor, *Purr ... Children's Book Illustrators Brag About Their Cats*, p. 21.

[138] Source: Walter Dean Myers, *Bad Boy: A Memoir*, p. 9.

[139] Source: Marilyn Hall and Rabbi Jerome Cutler, *The Celebrity Kosher Cookbook*, p. 130.

[140] Source: www.languagewrangler.com/article.php?sid=12. No longer available.

[141] Source: Kate Mostel and Madeline Gilford, *170 Years of Show Business*, p. 19.

[142] Source: Brian Alderson, *Ezra Jack Keats: Artist and Picture-Book Maker*, pp. 70-71.

[143] Source: Francoise Hudry, *Hugues Cuenod: With a Nimble Voice*, pp. 59-60.

[144] Source: Rose Heylbut and Aimé Gerber, *Backstage at the Opera*, p. 141.

[145] Source: Rosalynd Pflaum, *Marie Curie and Her Daughter Irene*, p. 117.

[146] Source: Herbert H. Breslin, editor, *The Tenors*, p. 170.

[147] Source: Henry C. Lahee, *Famous Singers of To-day and Yesterday*, pp. 74-75.

[148] Source: Brian Alderson, *Ezra Jack Keats: Artist and Picture-Book Maker*, p. 62.

[149] Source: Edward Edelson, *Funny Men of the Movies*, pp. 56, 58.

[150] Source: Joel Perry, *Funny That Way: Adventures in Fabulousness*, pp. 109-110.

[151] Source: Kate Clinton, *Don't Get Me Started*, p. 40.

[152] Source: Nigel Douglas, *More Legendary Voices*, p. 117.

[153] Source: Henry and Melissa Billings, *Eccentrics: 21 Stories of Unusual and Remarkable People*, p. 50.

[154] Source: Emma Albani, *Forty Years of Song*, pp. 203-204.

[155] Source: Herbert H. Breslin, editor, *The Tenors*, p. 10.

[156] Source: Marilyn Hall and Rabbi Jerome Cutler, *The Celebrity Kosher Cookbook*, p. 97.

[157] Source: Walter Slezak, *What Time's the Next Swan?*, p. 151.

[158] Source: Cal and Rose Samra, *Holy Hilarity*, pp. 29-30.

[159] Source: Judith Pinkerton Josephson, *Nikki Giovanni: Poet of the People*, p. 87.

[160] Source: Illaria Obidenna Ladré, *Illaria Obidenna Ladré: Memoirs of a Child of Theatre Street*, pp. 38-39.

[161] Source: Marco Perella, *Adventures of a No Name Actor*, pp. 200-202.

[162] Source: Dick Van Dyke, *Those Funny Kids!*, p. 40.

[163] Source: Rose Heylbut and Aimé Gerber, *Backstage at the Opera*, pp. 142-143.

[164] Source: George Zoritch, *Ballet Mystique: Behind the Glamour of the Ballet Russe*, p. 208.

[165] Source: Jay Leno, *Leading With My Chin*, pp. 250-252.

[166] Source: Joanna Cole, *On the Bus with Joanna Cole*, p. 48.

[167] Source: Jeff Sorensen, *Bob Newhart*, p. 75.

[168] Source: Doris Jadan, *The Great Life of Ivan Jadan*, pp. 25-26.

[169] Source: Lynda Pflueger, *Mark Twain: Legendary Writer and Humorist*, p. 67.

[170] Source: Henry and Melissa Billings, *Eccentrics: 21 Stories of Unusual and Remarkable People*, pp. 81-82.

[171] Source: William Oliver Stevens, *Famous Humanitarians*, p. 126.

[172] Roger Ebert, "Answer Man." 20 December 2004 <http://rogerebert.suntimes.com/apps/pbcs.dll/ section?category=ANSWERMAN>.

[173] Source: Jack Mingo, *The Juicy Parts*, p. 22.

[174] Source: Leonard S. Marcus, *A Caldecott Celebration: Six Artists and Their Paths to the Caldecott Medal*, p. 35.

[175] Source: Andrew Hecht, *Hollywood Merry-Go-Round*, p. 127.

[176] Source: Cath Carroll, *Tom Waits*, pp. 41-42.

[177] Source: Leslie Strudwick, *Athletes*, p. 40.

[178] Source: Noel Ross-Russell, *There Will I Sing*, p. 122.

[179] Source: Bob Dole, *Great Presidential Wit*, p. 52.

[180] Source: Andrew Hecht, *Hollywood Merry-Go-Round*, p. 128.

[181] Source: Maryann N. Weidt, *Oh, the Places He Went: A Story About Dr. Seuss*, pp. 26-27.

[182] Source: Richard Watson, *The Philosopher's Diet*, p. 121.

[183] Source: Maria Cole, *Nat King Cole: An Intimate Biography*, p. 72.

[184] Source: Dorothy Heiderstadt, *Painters of America*, p. 168.

[185] Source: Shimon Apisdorf, *Passover Survival Kit*, p. 9.

[186] Source: Walter Dean Myers, *Bad Boy: A Memoir*, pp. 9-10.

[187] Source: Margaret F. Atkinson and May Hillman, *Dancers of the Ballet*, pp. 10-11.

[188] Source: Veronica Vera, *Miss Vera's Cross-Dress for Success*, p. 112.

[189] Source: Marian Christy, *Marian Christy's Conversations: Famous Women Speak Out*, p. 120.

[190] Source: Deborah Kovacs, *Meet the Authors*, p. 52.

[191] Source: Leonard S. Marcus, *A Caldecott Celebration: Six Artists and Their Paths to the Caldecott Medal*, p. 25.

[192] Source: Gary Paulsen, *Woodsong*, pp. 43-47.

[193] Source: Julius Lester, *The Blues Singers: Ten Who Rocked the World*, pp. 32-33.

[194] Source: Mary Jane Matz, *Opera Stars in the Sun: Intimate Glimpses of Metropolitan Personalities*, p. 33.

[195] Source: Susan Bivin Aller, *J.M. Barrie: The Magic Behind Peter Pan*, pp. 49, 76-77.

[196] Source: Victoria Horne Oakie, compiler and editor, *"Dear Jack,"* p. 37.

[197] Source: Nathaniel Benchley, *Robert Benchley*, p. 10.

[198] Source: Robert Pegg, *Comical Co-Stars of Television*, p. 55.

[199] Source: George Zoritch, *Ballet Mystique: Behind the Glamour of the Ballet Russe*, p. 279.

[200] Source: Jack Mingo, *The Juicy Parts*, p. 53.

[201] Source: Laura Jimenez, *Hear Me OUT!: A Dose of Lesbian Humor for the Whole Human Race*, p. 132.

[202] Source: Avis Berman, *James McNeill Whistler*, p. 56.

[203] Source: Tom Verde, *Twentieth-Century Writers: 1950-1990*, p. 4.

[204] Source: Ron Knapp, *American Legends of Rock*, pp. 28, 30.

[205] Source: Deborah Kovacs and James Preller, *Meet the Authors and Illustrators*, p. 116.

[206] Source: Roger Ebert, "Bartleby," 24 May 2004 <www.suntimes.com/output/ebert1/wkp-news-bartleby24f.html>.

[207] Source: Robert L. Mott, *Radio Live! Television Live!*, pp. 115-116.

[208] Source: Joel Perry, *Funny That Way: Adventures in Fabulousness*, p. 23.

[209] Source: Sondra Henry and Emily Taitz, *Betty Friedan: Fighter for Women's Rights*, p. 65.

[210] Source: Barbara Kramer, *Amy Tan: Author of* The Joy Luck Club, pp. 59-60.

[211] Source: Marian Christy, *Marian Christy's Conversations: Famous Women Speak Out*, p. 121.

[212] Source: Howard Greenfeld, *Paul Gauguin*, pp. 10-11.

[213] Source: Rita Hunter, *Wait Till the Sun Shines, Nellie*, p. 44.

[214] Source: Cath Carroll, *Tom Waits*, p. 128.

[215] Source: Ron Knapp, *American Legends of Rock*, p. 39.

[216] Source: Geraldine Farrar, *Geraldine Farrar: The Story of an American Singer*, p. 4.

[217] Source: Raoul Abdul, *Famous Black Entertainers of Today*, p. 58.

[218] Source: Henry C. Lahee, *Famous Singers of To-day and Yesterday*, pp. 38-39.

[219] Source: Silvia Anne Sheafer, *Aretha Franklin: Motown Superstar*, p. 66.

[220] Source: Lynda Pflueger, *Mark Twain: Legendary Writer and Humorist*, pp. 33, 45-46, 90.

[221] Source: Margaret F. Atkinson and May Hillman, *Dancers of the Ballet*, pp. 115-116.

[222] Source: Victoria Horne Oakie, compiler and editor, *"Dear Jack,"* p. 117.

[223] Source: Darci Kistler, *Ballerina: My Story*, pp. 17-18.

[224] Source: Betsy Borns, *Comic Lives*, p. 109.

[225] Source: Rusty E. Frank, *Tap!*, p. 234.

[226] Source: Linda Jacobs, *Olga Korbut: Tears and Triumph*, p. 32.

[227] Source: Mary Jane Matz, *Opera Stars in the Sun: Intimate Glimpses of Metropolitan Personalities*, p. 46.

[228] Source: Gary Paulsen, *Woodsong*, pp. 22-25.

[229] Source: Mary Northrup, *American Computer Pioneers*, p. 77.

[230] Source: Amy Allison, *Antonio Banderas*, p. 44.

[231] Source: Anne E. Hill, *Ekaterina Gordeeva*, pp. 22-23.

[232] Source: Tom Powers, *Steven Spielberg: Master Storyteller*, p. 13.

[233] Source: Julius Lester, *The Blues Singers: Ten Who Rocked the World*, p. 44.

[234] Source: Perry Schwartz, *Carolyn's Story*, p. 33.

[235] Source: John Burke, *Rogue's Progress: The Fabulous Adventures of Wilson Mizner*, pp. 113-115, 118-119.

[236] Source: Tomie dePaola, *Here We All Are*, pp. 46, 56, 65-66.

[237] Source: Rusty E. Frank, *Tap!*, p. 139.

[238] Source: Tom Powers, *Steven Spielberg: Master Storyteller*, p. 16.

[239] Source: David McPhail, *In Flight with David McPhail*, pp. 34-36.

[240] Source: Sondra Henry and Emily Taitz, *Betty Friedan: Fighter for Women's Rights*, pp. 61-62.

[241] Source: Victor Seroff, *Renata Tebaldi: The Woman and the Diva*, pp. 163-164.

[242] Source: Dorothy Hamill, *On and Off the Ice*, pp. 60, 77.

[243] Source: Bill Littlefield, *Champions: Stories of Ten Remarkable Athletes*, pp. 95-96.

[244] Source: Ken Rappoport and Barry Wilner, *Girls Rule!*, pp. 88-89.

[245] Source: Pat Rediger, *Great African Americans in Sports*, p. 32.

[246] Source: Alyene Porter, *Papa was a Preacher*, p. 114.

[247] Source: Noel Ross-Russell, *There Will I Sing*, p. 93.

[248] Source: Jeff Sorensen, *Bob Newhart*, p. 74.

[249] Source: Rosalynd Pflaum, *Marie Curie and Her Daughter Irene*, p. 28.

[250] Source: Cal and Rose Samra, editors, *More Holy Humor*, p. 102.